# Fabulous Female Physicians

☆ THE WOMEN'S HALL OF FAME SERIES ☆

# Fabulous Female Physicians

by
SHARON KIRSH
with
FLORENCE KIRSH

Second
Story
Press

NATIONAL LIBRARY OF CANADA CATALOGUING IN PUBLICATION DATA

Kirsh, Sharon L. (Sharon Louise)
Fabulous female physicians

(The women's hall of fame series)
Includes bibliographical references.

ISBN 1-896764-43-6

1. Women physicians--Biography--Juvenile literature.
I. Kirsh, Florence  II. Title.  III. Series: Women's hall of fame series.

R692.K57 2001          j610'.92'2          C2001-902329-4

Edited by Charis Wahl
Cover design by Stephanie Martin
Text design by Laura McCurdy
Photo edit by Vivian Harrower

Printed and bound in Canada

*Second Story Press gratefully acknowledges the support of the Ontario
Arts Council and the Canada Council for the Arts for our publishing
program. We acknowledge the financial support of the Government of
Canada through the Book Publishing Industry Development Program.*

Published by
SECOND STORY PRESS
720 Bathurst Street, Suite 301
Toronto, ON
M5S 2R4
www.secondstorypress.on.ca

# ✫ Table of Contents ✫

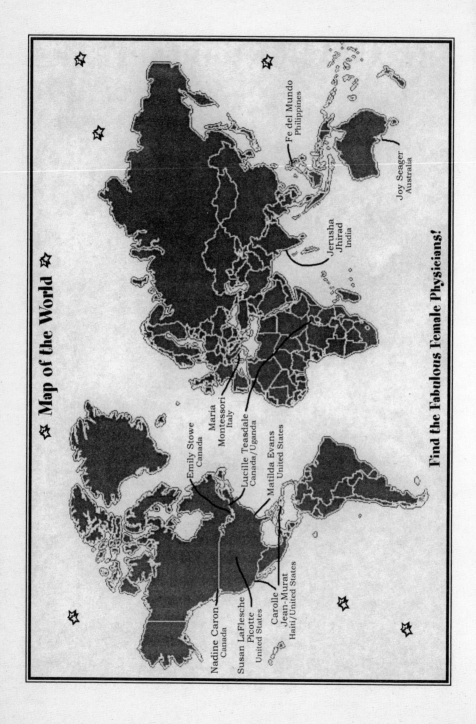

# ✧ Map of the World ✧

Find the Fabulous Female Physicians!

Fe del Mundo
Philippines

Joy Seager
Australia

Jerusha
Jhirad
India

Emily Stowe
Canada

Maria
Montessori
Italy

Lucille Teasdale
Canada/Uganda

Matilda Evans
United States

Nadine Caron
Canada

Susan LaFlesche
Picotte
United States

Carolle
Jean-Murat
Haiti/United States

6

# Introduction
## ✡ First Female ✡ Physicians

ACCORDING TO LEGEND, 2300 years ago a girl named Agnodice was born into a wealthy family in Athens, Greece. When she grew up, she decided to become a doctor. There was just one problem with her plan — Athenian women were forbidden to practice medicine, and could be executed if they disobeyed. So Agnodice left to study medicine in nearby Egypt, where women played an important role in the medical community. When she returned to Athens, she disguised herself as a man and began to treat patients.

Soon Agnodice saw that many women died of disease or during childbirth because they were embarrassed to be seen by a male doctor. She felt that she could no longer pretend, and confessed her secret to a woman who needed medical attention. The woman allowed Agnodice to treat her and was soon well again. Before long, many other women in Athens heard about the woman doctor disguised as a man, and they flocked to her for cures.

Then one day Agnodice's secret was discovered by some other doctors, who were quick to report her. During the trial a large group of her patients stormed into the court and demanded that the judges hear them. They explained that if

Agnodice were sentenced to death, then they would consider the men in the room to be their enemies. Some of the women even threatened to kill themselves if Agnodice died. The judges were shocked and frightened — the women were serious! Not only was Agnodice released, but the law was also changed. From then on, an Athenian woman could be a doctor as long as she treated only female patients.

Many people do not realize that women have been taking care of the sick for thousands of years. Throughout history women tried to figure out how the body works and what causes disease, and they concocted remedies from plants called herbs. Many were midwives, looking after pregnant women and helping them to deliver their babies. However, women were not usually welcomed as physicians. Agnodice won her fight, but other women's stories did not have a happy ending.

Jacqueline Felicie De Almania, known as Jacoba, lived in France almost 700 years ago. She practiced medicine in Paris without formal training, because only men could attend medical school at the time. In 1322 she was put on trial for practicing medicine because she was a woman. Several of her patients told the court about her great skills. The women claimed they would never have gone to a male doctor, and the men said that she was as skilled as any male physician. But the judges found Jacoba guilty and she was never allowed to practice again.

/ 🗋 ⚕

Nearly a millennium ago, a few women were able to make an impact on the medical world, however. For example, about 200 years before Jacoba's time a girl named Trotula was born into a noble family in Salerno, Italy. The medical school in that town was the best in Europe, and the only one to admit women. Trotula studied medicine and then taught at the school. She married a doctor and they had two sons who also became doctors. Together, the family wrote a medical encyclopedia.

Trotula was ahead of her time in her understanding of the human body and human emotions. She promoted a healthy diet, cleanliness and relaxation. Before she performed drastic surgery on a patient, she would try herbs and oils as a remedy. She also recommended that physicians approach their patients with gentleness and optimism. One of her most famous books is called *The Diseases of Women*. Male doctors used it for centuries to help them understand their female patients.

Ψ ۵ ✂

The practice of medicine has changed over time, and a great deal of progress has been made. For example, until about 100 years ago, most remedies were not very effective. Before 1940, there was no penicillin to cure infections caused by bacteria, and most babies born with a serious problem died soon after birth. Also, most aspiring female physicians had to go to special schools for women only, if they were permitted to study medicine at all.

The ten women you will meet in this book graduated from medical school. Even though they were born at different times and in different places, as you read about their lives you will see that they have much in common. They decided when they were quite young that they wanted to be some kind of doctor, and they worked very hard in high school and in medical school to become one. None was afraid to be thought odd or "unladylike" in her interests or ambitions. They were willing to make enormous sacrifices in order to reach their goals, and all of them bounced back from hardships.

Most cultures have at one time or another taught women that their place is in the home, that they are not smart enough to be physicians, and that it is not proper for women to examine men. There has also been discrimination based upon race or class. But the women in this book broke the rules. Each is a "first" — the first to do something no woman had done before in the field of medicine. They also worked to smooth the path for the women who would follow them. Many became involved in struggles with their government or with their university to change the laws and rules that held back women and other groups.

In many countries today, women are accepted into medical schools based on their merit as future physicians. This does not mean that all barriers have been removed. Certain types of medical practice are still considered better for men than for women — for example, there are few female surgeons. But times are changing, and sometime soon people might well wonder why a book was written about fabulous *female* physicians, because the world will be filled with them.

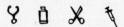

# ☆ 1 ☆

# Dr. Emily Stowe

1831      1903

OUTSIDE IN THE WINTRY NIGHT, feathery flakes of snow were gently falling. Inside, gathered around the light and warmth of the fireplace, sat a mother with her six daughters. The oldest was named Emily. Emily's mother was teaching her daughters their daily lessons — not how to cook, sew or make soap and candles because they already had these skills — but mathematics, literature and science. In the farming village of Norwich, Ontario, Canada in the 1840s, most girls did not learn such things. In fact, most girls did not go to school at all, and boys went only when they were not needed on the farm.

Emily's mother, Hannah Howard Jennings, had been sent to a Quaker boarding school in the United States when she was a girl. The Quakers, or the Society of Friends, are a Christian group formed in England in the 1600s. They believe that females and males should be equal — that both deserve a thorough education. (When Quakers came to America, they also spoke out against slavery.) Because she was a Quaker, Hannah educated her children even though they were girls.

*In 1871, a new law was passed that made school mandatory for children aged seven to eleven years old. But only for four months of the year!*

Hannah's garden was her crowning glory. It was filled with the plants she used in cooking, like peppermint, and others she used as cures for ailments, such as catnip, which was good for colds. Young Emily Jennings observed that her mother and other women were healers.

By age fifteen, Emily had done so well in her studies that she was hired to teach at a nearby school. (Teaching was one of the only jobs outside of the home available to unmarried women.) The school consisted of one room, one teacher, and children of all ages and ability levels. Emily had to teach her pupils as much as she could as quickly as she could, because by age twelve many would begin full-time jobs. For this hard work, she earned $170 per year, while male teachers in nearby schools earned $520 per year.

After seven years of teaching, Emily yearned to go to university. There was so much she wanted to learn, but she knew that as a woman she would not be accepted. Even so, she applied to the University of Toronto, six hours away by horse and carriage. There had to be a first time for everything!

Emily Jennings was not accepted at the university. Instead, she attended "normal school," where people learned how to teach elementary school. Graduates of normal school usually got better teaching jobs and more money than other teachers. An outstanding student, Emily was hired to be principal of Brantford Public School after her graduation in 1854. At the age of twenty-three, she was the first woman principal in Canada!

Then along came a carriage maker named John Stowe. He and Emily married in 1856 and had three children: Augusta, John Howard and Frank Jennings. Emily was delighted to be at home with her children because she believed that being a mother and homemaker gave women the power to shape the next generation.

Shortly after Frank was born in 1863, Emily's husband fell ill with tuberculosis (TB), a disease that requires a very long recovery period. John was sent to a special place to recuperate. In order to support her children and to pay the medical bills, Emily returned to teaching. Married women were not usually allowed to teach, but because Emily was close friends with the head of the Nelles Academy, a private school her daughter Augusta attended, she was offered a teaching position. Her wages were low and her evenings were filled with housework,

"Normal school" is not the opposite of "abnormal school." It comes from the French expression of 1839, école normale, which referred to the first school for teachers in France, serving as a model for how school should be taught.

childcare and lesson preparation. Cornelia, Emily's unmarried sister, offered to help with the household chores and to look after her young nephews.

When she visited John, Emily discovered that many women were dying unnecessarily because they believed it was improper for a woman to be examined by a male physician. Emily decided that *she* should become a physician, even though there was no such thing as a female doctor in Canada at the time. In her usual determined manner, she studied for her entrance exams while working and taking care of her children. When she had saved enough money for tuition and had passed the entrance exams, she applied to the University of Toronto Medical School.

She was not accepted. It was widely believed that female students would distract the male students and that it was wrong for men and women to examine naked bodies together. Besides, many people believed women could not possibly learn everything one must know to be a doctor, and that doctors' hours were too long and physically demanding for women, whose work was in the home.

Emily was not one to be discouraged. No medical school in Canada accepted women, but three schools in the United States did train women doctors. Emily chose the New York Medical College for Women because it specialized in plant remedies, like those she had learned from her mother.

New York was a huge city with more than one million residents, so noisy and crowded compared to rural Ontario. Emily's three children deeply missed their mother, but they were proud of her. And they did love Aunt Cornelia, who looked after them — she was kind and intelligent, and full of interesting stories.

What an outstanding day in 1867 when thirty-six-year-old Emily graduated from medical school in New York! She then moved the whole family to Toronto, a big city with a population of 50,000. Emily was now the first Canadian woman with a medical degree to practice medicine in Canada.

Just as the Stowes were settling into their new life, the Government of Ontario passed a law that all Canadian doctors who had gone to medical school in the United States had to attend at least one group of lectures at an Ontario medical school and write a special exam in order to practice medicine in Canada (to make sure that these new doctors had been trained to Canadian standards).

*Canada Post issued a stamp in Emily's honor!*

At first, Emily was not allowed to attend the lectures because she was female. But after two years of pleading, the medical school agreed to allow her and one other woman, Dr. Jennie Trout, to attend. Many of the professors and students mocked the two women and tried to embarrass them, but Emily and Jennie completed the course.

Emily's medical practice became large and successful. In 1873, after fully recovering, John became a dentist and set up shop in Emily's offices. Emily's ideas were ahead of her time; she understood the connection between cleanliness and eliminating germs, and between germs and illness, ideas that had been proved by Louis Pasteur in 1855 and Joseph Lister in 1865. She told her patients that frequent bathing, plenty of exercise, wholesome foods, little meat and no alcohol contribute to good health.

> The house that Emily's husband, John, built for the family near Brantford, Ontario, Canada was octagonal, like a stop sign!
> Some people believe this shape promotes peacefulness, and allows for the most light and wall space.

While Emily was a student in New York, she had become friends with a group of women who were speaking out in favor of giving women the right to vote. These early feminists — Elizabeth Cady Stanton, Susan B. Anthony and Lucretia Mott — fought for equal rights for women and against slavery. After Emily returned to Canada, she decided to fight for Canadian women's rights. There was a lot to fight for. Women could not vote in any election. Married women could not own property. Mothers had no say in their children's upbringing; only fathers had the power to make big decisions such as sending children away to work, giving them up for adoption, educating them (or not) and choosing their religion. If you were a girl, then your education was not as good as any boy's, no matter how smart you were.

Several women joined together with Emily as their leader to fight these unfair laws. They gave themselves a surprising name: the Toronto Women's Literary Club! But instead of discussing their favorite books, these women met once a week to talk about better working conditions for poor women, better schooling for girls, improved healthcare for women, and enfranchisement — full citizenship, including the right to vote. As long as women did not have the right to vote for the members of government, or to be members of the government themselves, they were less than full citizens.

Soon the women of the "Literary Club" decided that enough was enough! They wanted society to know exactly what they stood for, so they changed their name in 1883 to the Toronto Women's Suffrage Association. Their main goal was to win the vote for all women.

Meanwhile, Emily's daughter, Augusta, pursued her own medical career. In 1879 Augusta was the first woman to be accepted into Victoria College in Toronto to study medicine. At first, some professors and students picked on her, but she gradually won their respect. When she accepted her diploma in 1883, it is said that her fellow students jumped to their feet and cheered. One classmate did more than cheer; John Gullen asked her to marry him. Their marriage — the first between two Canadian doctors — lasted sixty years, until Augusta's death in 1943.

*Suffrage is the right to vote; a suffragist is a person who advocates for this right, especially for women, and a suffragette is a woman who advocates suffrage for women.*

Because women in Ontario were still not entirely welcome in medical school, as evidenced by Augusta's experience, Emily and the Women's Suffrage Association also fought for a women's medical college to train women to become doctors in an atmosphere of respect. In 1883, the Woman's Medical College (later renamed the Ontario Medical College for Women) welcomed its first students. The college created a clinic where women patients were treated by female physicians. That clinic grew to become Toronto's well-known Women's College Hospital.

Emily's husband, John, had stood beside her through all her triumphs and challenges. When he died in 1891, Emily moved in with her son Frank and his wife, who lived next door to her daughter, Augusta, and her husband. Two years later, Emily retired from medicine but remained president of the Dominion Women's Enfranchisement Association, continuing to demand women's right to vote. When Emily died on April 30, 1903, at age seventy-two, women throughout Canada and the United States expressed their grief.

Although Emily did not live to see women vote, her daughter Augusta Stowe-Gullen carried on the fight. On April 12, 1917, the women of Ontario were granted suffrage in provincial and city elections. A year later, Canadian women aged twenty-one and over won the right to vote for Members of Parliament in federal elections. Augusta, the first woman to graduate from a previously men-only Canadian medical school, became a professor and eventually the director of the Ontario Medical College for Women.

Emily Jennings Stowe and Augusta Stowe-Gullen struggled against tough odds to win an equal place for women in medicine and in all of society. Hannah Howard Jennings' belief in education for her daughters had a strong impact — two of Emily's sisters became doctors, too!

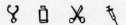

# 2

# Dr. Susan LaFlesche Picotte

1865       1915

SUSAN WAS TIRED, hot and thirsty. Since sunrise she had been riding from village to village on the Omaha Indian reservation in Nebraska, and now even her horse was exhausted. They had been stopping at every home where someone was sick. So many people and so many serious illnesses: tuberculosis, cholera, dysentery and influenza.

Susan LaFlesche was the only doctor for the 1300 Omaha. She had been the tribe's doctor for four years, braving sharp winter winds, snow and scorching summer sun to reach her patients. Her ears and face had begun to hurt all the time, probably from long exposure to the winter cold on horseback, but her only concern was for those who needed her. Susan LaFlesche was the first Native American woman physician.

Her story began with her three sisters and one half-brother. She was the youngest of the five, the child of Mary and Joseph LaFlesche. Her father was known as Iron Eye, and he was the Chief of the Omaha. Until the time of Susan's birth the Omaha had been a hunting tribe, because the prairie had been filled with millions of buffalo. Young girls learned how to preserve buffalo meat for the winter months, and how to create clothes, moccasins and tipis from buffalo skins. Boys learned how to hunt and how to make weapons for hunting.

In 1850, there were 50 million buffalo on the plains. In 1883, there were only 50 buffalo!

In 1862 the United States government offered free land (160-acre farms) to any family — *except* Native families — if they would come out West to farm. The government gave away millions of acres to white settlers from the eastern United States and from France, Germany, Switzerland and Sweden. This created two problems for the Omaha. First, much of this "free" land already belonged to Native Americans, including the Omaha. Second, by 1880 the settlers had shot so many buffalo that the Omaha had nothing left to hunt. The government agreed to send cattle to replace the buffalo, but often the cattle did not arrive.

Chief Iron Eye saw that this was the end of the Omaha's

traditional way of life. He urged his people to cultivate their fertile prairie land — to grow grain, corn, potatoes, beans, squash and melons. He asked them to build wooden houses and to give up their earth-covered lodges and skin tipis. He also taught them about the harmful effects of the alcohol that white settlers were selling. Some settlers even gave free samples of whiskey to Omaha children so they, too, would want to buy more and more.

Many tribespeople disagreed strongly with Iron Eye. They believed that he had given up too easily, signing away a lot of land in exchange for a small reservation. Now, instead of enough buffalo to hunt and eat, instead of traditional prayers, earth lodges and tipis, the Omaha had only a few buffalo, white settlers' diseases and alcohol.

But Joseph and Mary saw that their five children would have to deal with the white people, and thought it was important that they receive an education in both Native and white peoples' cultures. Susan attended the government-owned Omaha Agency School, a three-mile walk from her home, where she learned English. In 1879, at age fourteen, she and her sister Marguerite were sent far from home to the Institute for Young Ladies in Elizabeth, New Jersey. Their older sister, Susette, had already graduated from the Institute.

After her graduation three years later, Susan returned to her reservation to teach at its mission school. She was only

A "mission school" is a school run by a religious organization in order to spread its beliefs to students. Susan's school was run by the Presbyterian Church. There, students learned about white culture and Christianity, and learned to speak English. Susan's native language was "Umonhon," which means "against the current."

seventeen years old, but could clearly see the problems in her community. She understood that families who had lived as hunters could not easily switch to a farming life, and many people went hungry much of the time. She saw that her people did not receive adequate health care from the doctors sent by the government. Many of their new illnesses came from white settlers and from their foods, which the Omaha were forced to eat because the buffalo were gone. She knew that alcohol caused problems not only for the person who drank, but also for the whole family and for the community.

A bold idea came to Susan: she would become a doctor for her people. The Omaha had medicine men and women who used prayers and sweat baths and potions made of herbs, but there were no Native doctors — and certainly no female Native doctors — who had trained in a white peoples' medical school. But first, she had to do more studying. At age nineteen, she and two of her sisters received scholarships to the Hampton Normal and Agricultural Institute in Virginia. This school had opened in 1868 to educate newly-freed slaves, but by 1884 it also accepted Native Americans. Susan graduated second in her class in 1886, and received a gold medal for high scholastic achievement.

In 1889, the year Susan earned her medical degree, Carlos Montezuma of the Yavapavi became the first Native male to graduate as a doctor. Both went on to work in their reservation communities.

At that time a poor Native woman could hardly expect to be accepted into a white peoples' medical school, but Susan applied anyway. As it turned out, the Women's

Medical College of Pennsylvania could not ignore her brilliant academic record. The Women's National Indian Association granted her a scholarship, and she went east yet again. For three years she studied hard, made many new friends and volunteered to visit orphanages filled with Native children. Her head spun with the contrast between the wealth and beauty of Philadelphia and the poverty and troubles of her people.

Susan (center) with members of her family.

In 1888, at the beginning of her third year of college, Susan's father died. It must have been painful for her, knowing the pride he would have had in his daughter, doctor to the Omaha!

For four years after her graduation she traveled to sick patients, no matter the weather, no matter how exhausted she was. Sometimes she brought them food because they were almost starving. She also set up an office in her house in the town of Macy, Nebraska, where she had attended the Agency school. People came to her for cures and advice, and she was wise and gentle. She asked herself, "How can we better ourselves?" She encouraged everyone else to ask that question, too. When she was only twenty-eight, her poor health forced her to stop traveling. Two male doctors took over, but often asked for her advice.

Around this time she met a farmer named Henry Picotte. Although Susan had always said she would never marry, Henry won her over. They married in 1894 and moved to Bancroft on the Omaha reservation. Soon they had two sons, Caryl and Pierre. Susan's life was hectic: she was the town physician, treating both Native people and white people; she looked after her ailing mother, who lived with her; and she was an adviser, translator, teacher and the mother of two young boys.

"Prohibition" means laws making it illegal to make, sell or buy alcohol. From the mid-1800s to the 1930s, many women fought for such laws because their husbands often spent their pay in the taverns while the family went without proper food and clothing. Most prohibition laws were cancelled during the 1930s.

Like her father, Susan struggled to teach her people about the evils of alcohol. It was frustrating to stand by while white traders sold liquor to the Omaha. Even at home Susan could not escape the problem. When her husband Henry died in 1905, it may well have been from an alcohol-related illness. She missed him terribly.

Now a single mother, Susan, her sons and her mother moved to Walthill, a new town on their reservation. Susan's sister Marguerite lived there, and soon the two of them were busy organizing religious and community activities.

By this time Susan had become the unofficial leader of her people, intelligently and calmly connecting the Native world and the white world. As a member of the State Medical

Association she led a group to Washington, DC, demanding a new law that would prohibit the sale of alcohol in any town on the Omaha or neighboring Winnebago reservations. In 1906 the law was passed.

Susan became the county health officer and went to the Nebraska State government to demand better public health laws. Her people needed good medical care, and the government must provide for all its citizens, not just for white people.

On February 7, 1887, the Omaha were granted American citizenship. It was not until 1924 that all Native Americans officially became citizens!

In the back of Susan's mind, an idea had been growing for several years. Why not build a hospital right on the reservation? Her own mother had died at home in 1909, but many sick tribespeople had to travel to hospitals in white towns, where they often died alone in a strange environment. With determination, she managed to raise $10,000 from the people of Walthill. The hospital was built, and Susan became its head. It was filled with sunshine, and had a large open porch with hammocks that allowed patients to bask in the fresh air. Both Native and white people were treated at Susan's hospital.

Some people believe that by 1915, after twenty-five years of doctoring, Dr. Susan LaFlesche Picotte had cared for every one of the 1300 members of her tribe at one time or another. At night she had kept the lamp lit in her window in case her patients needed her. During most of this time she suffered from the bone disease that had caused severe pain in her ear and face. She underwent surgery, but it did not help. Sadly, she died at age fifty and was buried in Bancroft, where she had lived with Henry. Her sons were only seventeen and nineteen years old.

Throughout her life Susan tried to combine her traditional ways and the customs of the white society in which she had received her education and training. She showed respect for both cultures, and used both modern and traditional medicine. At her funeral a Presbyterian minister conducted the service, but the closing prayer was offered by a Native elder in the Omaha language.

If you go to Walthill, Nebraska today, you will find Susan's hospital, renamed in her memory. In the late 1940s it became a care center for the elderly, and after that a family health clinic. In 1989 the building was restored. Today it is called the Susan LaFlesche Picotte Center, and displays photos and objects from her life. It was declared a National Historic Landmark in 1993.

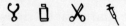

# 3

# Dr. Matilda Arabelle Evans

**1872**        **1935**

I**N THE HEAT OF THE SUN,** Matilda and her parents picked cotton. Life was harsh in Aiken, South Carolina, USA. Matilda was the oldest of Andy and Harriet's three children. Just ten years before she was born, President Abraham Lincoln had called for the freeing of Black slaves in the United States, but Black people were still doing the toughest jobs, at the lowest wages. Andy and Harriet dreamed of education for their children so that the next generation could rise above their poverty. For most Black families this remained a dream.

After slavery officially ended, the Pennsylvanian Freedmen's Association built several schools for Black children. One of these, the Martha Schofield Industrial School, opened in South Carolina in 1868. Matilda, a very energetic and intelligent girl, became a student there. Sensing a special spark in Matilda, Miss Schofield encouraged her to apply to Oberlin College in Ohio, even though it was unheard-of for a fifteen-year-old Black girl to go off to college. Matilda was accepted!

In her first few months at Oberlin, Matilda did so well in her studies that the college gave her free tuition for the next four years. In order to pay for her other expenses, she worked in the college dining hall during the school term, and in the summers went back home to can fruit. Matilda graduated in 1891.

For a brief time she taught at the Martha Schofield Industrial School, but Miss Schofield encouraged her to apply to medical school. In gratitude for her support, Matilda later wrote a biography of this important educator, which was published in 1916. Because of her outstanding record at Oberlin, Matilda was accepted at the Women's Medical College of Pennsylvania in Philadelphia. The school had been founded by the Quakers in 1850, and Matilda was the only Black graduate in 1897.

After medical school Matilda moved back to South Carolina. She was the first Black woman to practice medicine in that state. She settled in Columbia, the capital city. Half of the 50,000 people in Columbia were Black, yet there were no hospitals for them, no training schools for Black nurses and almost no doctors who would treat Black patients. Matilda was going to change all that!

Because she was the only female doctor in Columbia, many women flocked to her. Usually the white patients could pay her for her services, and this made up for the Black patients who could not afford to. Soon she became a well-known doctor and surgeon.

Matilda opened her house to many Black patients, and it became a makeshift hospital until she could raise enough money to start a twenty-five-bed hospital. In 1901 the Taylor Lane Hospital opened with Matilda, not yet thirty years old, as its head. A training program for nurses offered Black women a chance for a good job. Unfortunately fire destroyed the Taylor Lane Hospital, but Matilda was not discouraged. She raised enough money to build the St. Luke's Hospital and Training School for Nurses.

Because she was an outstanding physician and community organizer, Matilda was elected to head several medical organizations. For example, she was president of the Palmetto State Medical Society and vice-president of the National Medical Association, positions not usually given to women. The Richland Memorial Hospital also named an award for her.

Step by step, Matilda filled the gaps in the medical care available to the Black community. She loved to be around young people and she knew that many poor children did not receive medical care. She convinced school authorities to let her perform free physical examinations of Black children in the schools. Just as she had suspected, among these inadequately nourished children she found countless cases of infected tonsils, rotten teeth, ringworm and scabies. Matilda convinced the school boards to have regular physical examinations in the schools, including immunization against certain diseases. Children's lives were improved — some saved — through her school program.

In the basement of a church, Matilda then started the Zion Baptist Church Clinic. On the first day, 700 patients showed up! Soon the clinic moved to a larger space, where Black people could receive free medical care provided by an ear, eye, nose and throat specialist, a dentist, and by Matilda, who gave vaccines to children.

In order to educate people about good health practices, personal cleanliness and how to prepare food safely, Matilda started the Good Health Association of South Carolina. It spread the word all through the state: cleanliness means less disease.

Matilda's love of children did not stop with caring for their health. She turned her farmhouse, called Cottage Inn, into a haven for eleven children. Five were children of relatives who had died. The other children had been left at her office by parents who could not raise them. Matilda officially adopted seven of these children, and all eleven went to college.

On Matilda's farm was a pond. She is said to have taught herself to swim by reading instructions written by a sea captain. Once she knew how to stay afloat, she opened her pond to local children and taught hundreds of them how to swim. Matilda also enjoyed dancing and playing the piano. She loved to have fun, and most of all, she loved children. At age sixty-three, Matilda died and was buried in the Palmetto Cemetery in Columbia.

Matilda Arabelle Evans treated thousands of women, men, and children. Without her, they may never have seen a doctor, had an operation or received a vaccination against preventable diseases. She was a dedicated humanitarian, whose love of life brought love *and* life to many people.

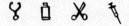

☆ **4** ☆

# Dr. Maria Montessori

1870          1952

TWELVE-YEAR-OLD MARIA and her mother, Renilde, had a secret: Maria wanted to go to a technical school to study mathematics. What a strange idea it seemed at the time, wanting to learn a boys' subject in a boys' school! A girl, in Rome in 1882, studying something other than Greek and Latin and literature? Renilde understood her only child. She was well educated for a woman of her time, and she wanted her daughter to stretch as far as she could.

But Maria's father, Alessandro, wanted his beautiful daughter to learn "womanly" arts, like piano, needlework and languages, and to marry a wealthy man. When Renilde and Maria told him of their plan for technical school, Alessandro exploded, "A mathematician! Technical school!" It took much pleading before he granted Maria her wish.

At technical school, Maria soon realized that even interesting subjects could be very boring. The problem was with the way things were taught — sitting at desks, repeating rules, memorizing facts. Still, Maria was an outstanding mathematics student and talked about becoming an engineer. Alessandro was alarmed by his self-confident and rebellious child. If she had to have a job, he thought, why couldn't she be a teacher like other unmarried young women? Maria said that a teacher was the *last* thing she wanted to be.

When she graduated from technical school, she announced that she had changed her mind. Forget engineering; she wanted to be a doctor. Renilde was excited — her daughter would be the first female doctor in modern Italy! After much shouting, Alessandro gave in. He did not approve, but he would not stand in her way. Besides, no woman had ever been accepted to medical school, so there was not much to worry about. But when Maria completed her degree in math and science at the University of Rome, she *was* accepted to medical school!

Because she was the only woman in her class, Maria ran into many obstacles. For example, it was considered improper for a man and a woman to handle a naked body together, so during anatomy class she was not allowed to cut up the bodies with her classmates. Instead, she had to go into the lab alone at night and teach herself. The lab smelled of the chemicals used to preserve organs, such as brains and kidneys, in jars. Shelves of skulls and bones surrounded her. Often she felt frightened and sick, but she was determined to become a doctor so she kept at it.

As a young female, Maria was not supposed to walk outdoors unescorted. Her father had to walk her to and from school every day, which was awkward since he was already angry that she was not respecting his wishes by becoming a doctor. When she arrived, she had to wait until all the male students had been seated before she could enter the lecture hall, because females were forbidden to mingle with men in the hallway.

Sixteen-year-old Maria in 1886.

At first, several classmates pulled pranks and told jokes to humiliate her. But as time went by, the young men learned to respect Maria. After four years of general medicine she decided to study pediatrics (childhood medicine) and psychiatry (the study of mental illness) for two years. Meanwhile, she worked part-time at a children's hospital.

Maria graduated in 1896, her final grade an amazing 100 out of 105. She was now *dottoressa*, a female doctor, the first in Italy.

She opened a medical clinic, treating mostly children. She also continued to work at the University of Rome's psychiatric clinic. This required her to visit asylums, or hospitals for people with mental illness. Until modern times, these places were often more like prisons than hospitals.

In the asylums, Maria found children who were mentally slow or who had complicated behavioral problems. All day they sat around with nothing to do — no toys, no school, no affection. They did not know how to read or write or play. Maria could not stop thinking about them, and decided that what they needed was schooling, but not the boring kind she had experienced. First they must learn through their senses — sight, hearing, taste, touch and smell — and then learn through their minds.

One of her co-workers at the psychiatric clinic, Dr. Giuseppe Montesano, also wanted to help the asylum children. Maria and Giuseppe fell in love and, in 1898, Maria had a baby named Mario Montessori. Maria hid the pregnancy and the baby from everyone except her parents and close friends. If the public found out that she was an unmarried woman with a baby, Maria would be shamed and no one would want her as their doctor.

Baby Mario was sent to live with a family in the countryside near Rome, to be raised as their child. No one knows why Maria and Giuseppe did not marry; but they promised each other that they would never marry anyone else and that they would keep their son a secret. Maria often visited Mario, but he did not know that she was his birth mother.

> **Modern Montessori schools build upon Maria's idea that a child's unique personality develops through exploration with materials and activities, and interaction with peers.**

In 1899, Maria and Giuseppe were asked to direct a training school for teachers who planned to work with children like those in the asylum. Here was Maria's chance to test her ideas. With great energy she began making teaching materials — beads, blocks and laces in many colors, shapes, sizes and textures. Soon the school was a beehive of activity, with children learning through all their senses. The students were respected by their teachers, and they felt special. This was not like the asylum, where they had been bored and neglected. After a short time, they began to read and write, and to smile. When Maria took them to a public school for the regular students' reading and writing tests, they passed! This made her wonder what would happen if she tried her new approach with regular students.

Suddenly, in 1901, Maria quit her job. Perhaps because Giuseppe broke their agreement and married another woman, Maria could no longer work with him. She decided to go back to research. It seemed that children liked to learn and did not need to be forced. She studied subjects that would help her understand how children learn.

As a doctor and as an educator, she could picture a school where the teacher's job was to gently ask questions that encourage children to think, not just to memorize. At such a school, children would feel at home. They would learn through physical education, through their senses, through drawing and music. Maria found that, on the one hand, all children go through the same stages of development (for example learning to walk before learning to skip) and, on the other hand, every child is unique or one of a kind.

A golden opportunity to test her ideas came along in 1906 when an apartment building in Rome was fixed up for very poor families. Soon after the families moved in, the owners became annoyed with the children who were damaging the building while their parents were at work. Something had to be done, so the owners invited Maria to open a children's room in the building to keep them out of trouble.

In January 1907, the room was opened. Maria called it *Casa dei Bambini*, Italian for "Children's House." On the first day her fifty students, ages three to six, filed into the peaceful, orderly, colorful room. They were shy and frightened. Some of them were crying, but before long they could tell that this was a safe place.

Because Maria had patients to see, she could not be at the Children's House all day. She hired a teacher, but every day Maria came to see her students and to figure out how to make this the best place to learn.

What a magical place it was! Unlike other schoolrooms, the Children's House had chairs and tables that were small enough for three-year-olds and light enough that the smallest children could move them by themselves. There were little sinks the children could reach to wash their hands and low, open shelves with toys and books, rather than locked closets that only the teacher was allowed to touch. On the windowsills and tabletops sat plants, flowers and fishbowls. Outside there was a garden, where children could plant things and feel like a part of Nature.

Maria was given the nickname "Mammolina," Italian for "darling mama." This reflected her patience, warmth and intelligence.

Instead of having the teacher responsible for everything, every child had jobs such as feeding the fish, tidying the classroom or serving lunch. These "exercises of practical life" taught the children responsibility and made them feel competent. Every child was respected by the teacher and by the other children.

Before long the four- and five-year-olds began to read and write. The teacher had not taught them — she had given them cutouts of letters to play with and had told them the letter sound when they asked. They began to notice words all around them. Six months after the opening, word had spread around the world about these poorly clothed, dirty children who had come to life. Maria said they had revealed their true souls.

More "children's houses" opened in Italy. Maria spoke publicly about how children learn, and her ideas spread to other countries, such as Canada, the United States, Australia, England, China, Spain and Holland. Italy and Switzerland started to use her approach in every school. In 1909, she wrote a book called *The Montessori Method*, and within three years it had been translated into twenty languages. By age forty, Maria wanted to spend all of her time training teachers and helping to start new schools, so she gave up her medical practice.

When her mother died in 1912, Maria was devastated. Renilde had been her greatest source of support, and Maria had lived with her parents throughout adulthood.

Not long after, however, something lifted Maria's spirits. When Mario was fifteen, he told her that he believed she was his biological mother. She admitted the truth, and he decided to live with her. For the remainder of her life, even after Mario married and had children, he worked closely with Maria in establishing new schools.

Mario and Maria moved several times, and lived in the United States during World War I (1914–1918). By 1934, when the Italian dictator, Mussolini, was in power, they were forced to leave Italy again because Maria had openly spoken out against his politics. She believed that children were the hope for the future. In her schools, there was respect for differences — in the way people learned and in the way they looked. There was respect for the environment, and everyone felt special. This kind of tolerance did not suit Mussolini's own ideas, and as a punishment, he closed all her schools. Hitler did the same in Germany. During World

War II (1939–1945), Maria and Mario lived in India. After the war they traveled and lectured, making Holland (the Netherlands) their main home.

In 1949, 1950 and 1951, Maria Montessori was given a most special honor. She was nominated three times for the Nobel Peace Prize.

By the time she died in Holland at age eighty-two, there were thousands of Montessori schools in fifty countries. Of all the children she had known and loved, the one dearest to her was Mario. When she died she let the world know their true relationship: in her will, she left all her possessions to Mario, "my son."

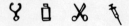

## 5

# Dr. Jerusha Jhirad

1891        1984

JERUSHA, her sister Leah and their cousins sat in the Indian sun chewing sweet, red coffee berries. Their laughter was surrounded by the quiet, familiar sounds of cows, goats and birds, and the creaking of pulleys as water buckets dipped in and out of the well. When the children grew hot, they raced to the cool stream that ran through the coffee estate their father managed for the owner, his father-in-law. All year long, they watched the vegetable garden grow, with its tomatoes, chilies and pumpkins, and when their mother needed herbs for cooking, they picked the coriander, curry leaves, mint and parsley.

Jerusha and Leah were close in spirit and only fifteen months apart in age. During the week, their mother prepared the girls for the day when they would go to boarding school like their two older sisters and their brother. She taught Jerusha and Leah to read and write Marathi (the local language), as well as arithmetic and the basic beliefs of Judaism. In the evening, their father tested their knowledge and taught them prayers.

Friday night, the beginning of the Jewish Sabbath, was a magical time for Jerusha, especially when all of her siblings gathered at home. Father blessed each of his children, and Mother served a festive meal in an atmosphere of love and support. The family discussed ideas, including their religious beliefs. They were members of the Bene-Israel, a group of Jews thought to be one of the Twelve Lost Tribes of Israel, who had arrived in India two thousand years earlier.

When the time came for Jerusha to make the four-day journey to boarding school in Poona, she kissed her family goodbye and wandered the estate one last time. Little did she realize that she would never see it again.

At boarding school her mind blossomed. With her extraordinary memory and determination, she eagerly gobbled up literature, mathematics, history and geography, and earned a reputation as the student who helped others to learn. More than anything, she wanted to make her mother proud of her. Despite being very busy, she missed her family.

Soon after Jerusha left for boarding school, disaster hit the coffee estate. An insect called "planter's pest" attacked the shrubs, and the land had to be abandoned. Father found work with the railways, and Mother, Leah and the new baby, Ellis, moved to Pune. Before long, Mother was diagnosed with rheumatoid arthritis, a sometimes crippling disease. She needed assistance and Leah, although highly talented in art and music, had to stay home to help her.

The following year, Jerusha's seventeen-year-old sister, Miriam, became pregnant with twins. The pregnancy did not go well, and Miriam became seriously ill. Her life was saved by a woman, Dr. Benson, who was the head of Cama Hospital for Women in Bombay, a hospital staffed entirely by women. When Jerusha heard the whole story, including the loss of the twins, she was deeply moved. Someday, she thought, she too would become a doctor and save women's lives. She too would be the head of Cama Hospital.

Jerusha's father had begun medical studies himself, but when he was eighteen he married Jerusha's mother, who was only fourteen years old! Jerusha's father had to stop going to school to support his new family. Marrying early was common. Shortly after Jerusha left for boarding school at about age eleven, her two older sisters left school to marry at the ages of sixteen and seventeen.

At first Jerusha's grandfather had paid her school tuition, but soon she had won enough scholarships to pay her own way. There was no money left over, however, and now that Jerusha's father was a railway employee, the family could not afford luxuries. When one of her closest school friends married, Jerusha had to miss the wedding because she did not have extra money for an appropriate saree.

Miriam and her husband, Jacob, lived with his parents. One day Jacob's married sister came home to give birth to her child. Just after her baby was born, she began to bleed heavily. The midwife and nurse could not stop the bleeding — a doctor had to be called, but all doctors were men. Jacob's mother, typical of her culture and time, would not allow the doctor to enter her daughter's bedroom. He could only shout instructions to the nurse and midwife from behind a closed door. Jacob's sister died, and again Jerusha was struck by the need for women doctors to help Indian women.

After graduating from high school with a brilliant record, she was admitted to medical school in Bombay. There were few women at the school, and they became fast friends. Most were Parsee (originally Persian), a few were Hindu or Christian, and Jerusha was the only Jew. Religious custom did not yet allow Muslim women to become doctors. Jerusha and her school friends liked to gather at her home where Mother, confined to a wheelchair, entertained them with her laughter and motherly advice. Leah and Ellis, too, enjoyed the company of the young medical students.

Jerusha graduated in 1912, winning most of the prizes. Tiny in size but grand in knowledge and energy, at twenty-one Jerusha was the first woman in the Bene-Israel community to become a doctor.

Some of the Bene-Israel women organized a gathering to celebrate Jerusha's accomplishment. It was so relaxed and pleasant that Jerusha suggested they meet regularly, perhaps once a month. At that time, women married young and often lived with in-laws. They were socially isolated from other women and, in the company of men, had to be quiet and serious. The idea of meeting with a group of women, to share experiences and to have a good time, was appealing.

Jerusha worked hard to create *Stree Mandal,* a women's association. The association held daily afternoon classes in cooking, languages, needlework and sewing for women whose schooling had been cut short by marriage or poverty. On Saturdays they read the Bible and studied religious ideas. Some of the Bene-Israel women used the skills they learned, for example sewing clothes, to start small businesses. When Muslim women heard of the daily classes, they asked if they could participate. Soon *Stree Mandal* welcomed all women.

Many of Jerusha's patients were wives of Arab merchants in Bombay. Because they would see a female physician only, Jerusha became well known. With her income she paid for someone to help her mother so that Leah could pursue her passion for art and violin, and Ellis could attend a boys' school and play sports.

But she still had her secret dream: heading Cama Hospital and dedicating her life to women and children, just as Dr. Benson had done. Jerusha applied to further her education in London, England. She became the first Indian woman to be awarded a Government of India Scholarship, an honor previously reserved for men who were studying abroad. She studied obstetrics and gynecology at the London School of Medicine for Women, and then worked at the Elizabeth Garrett Anderson Hospital. The hospital was named for the first female to qualify as a doctor in Britain (in 1870).

Jerusha had picked a dangerous time to live in England. World War I was raging, and there were nightly air raids on London by the Germans. When the alarm sounded, hospital staff had to rush patients into shelters. Some patients could not be moved easily, and everyone was terrified. One day Jerusha was startled by an enormous crashing sound that shook the whole hospital. The building next door had been bombed and was on fire!

In 1919 she returned to Bombay with an MD in obstetrics and gynecology from the University of London — a first for an Indian woman. It had been five long years since she had left home, and at age twenty-eight, she was less shy and more confident than she had ever been.

Her greatest thrill was to be reunited with her mother, whose arthritis had become even worse. But her mother's twisted hands had not prevented her from writing long letters to Jerusha, keeping her informed about her ever-expanding family. More nieces and nephews had been born, Ellis had become a college student, and her father had retired and was living at home.

*Jerusha's mother's sister had been the first university graduate among the Bene-Israel women, and Jerusha's cousin had been second. Jerusha was third, and the first to become a doctor. Her mother's father, a civil engineer, had been the first male university graduate in the community.*

Lady Hardinge Medical College in Delhi was a women's college for medical studies. All of the teachers were women, and most of them were British. Jerusha took a teaching post there, always reminding future doctors that Indian women would rather die than be examined by a male doctor. She believed that all people, regardless of color or class, should be treated equally and with dignity. Being rich or British should not make a patient special, but to many of the teachers at the college, it did.

When asked to be the Medical Officer of a hospital in Bangalore, she accepted. There she developed services for pregnant women, teaching nurses and midwives the importance of checkups during pregnancy. Some of her wealthier patients donated money to build a labor room and an operating room, and to buy equipment. In addition, Jerusha raised money for new-baby and gynecological clinics. Because her patients loved her, many of them volunteered to work in the hospital with sick patients or with new mothers.

Jerusha's family had come to live with her in Bangalore, but when her mother died Jerusha decided to return to Bombay with her father. Her mother had been her inspiration, showing through example a quiet strength and dignity.

Leah, no longer needed to help at home, went off to London to study art.

> **Jerusha continued to keep in touch with her nieces and nephews throughout her life. Three nieces and one nephew had become doctors themselves!**

In 1925, Jerusha was given an honorary post at the Cama Hospital. She started a private practice for those who could pay, and worked for free at Cama. Her modesty and humility guided her. She spoke directly and to the point, and she dressed simply, in a plain white saree with a watch and two thin gold bangles on her wrist.

While in England Jerusha had learned about Liberal Judaism, a new form of Judaism that was adapted to modern times. Women were allowed to participate in the service in ways that had been closed to them in traditional Judaism. When she returned to India, she introduced these ideas to some members of her community and together they created the Jewish Religious Union and eventually started a reform synagogue called *Rodef Shalom*. She and Leah devoted much of their time to organizing a choir and activities for Jewish teenagers in the congregation.

Three years later, in 1928, her childhood dream came true: she was appointed Medical Officer-in-charge of Cama Hospital, the first Indian woman to earn this position. Just as Dr. Benson had saved her sister Miriam's life, so she could now help other women. For twenty years she worked to improve the hospital's medical facilities and to educate women to better their lives and those of their children. When Cama was celebrating its Golden Jubilee (50th birthday) in 1936, Jerusha orchestrated a fundraising effort that collected enough money to build an outpatient department, a home for resident nurses and one for doctors, and a hostel for post-graduate students.

Jerusha knew that she and her staff should be aware of new information. She subscribed to several medical journals and eventually persuaded the government to give grants

 **Dr. Jerusha Jhirad on the grounds of Cama Hospital in 1947.**

for subscriptions. Years later, in celebration of her eightieth birthday, a post-graduate library was established at Cama in her name.

In 1953, she and Leah moved to a quiet village near Bombay called Dahisar. There were no streetlights and only well water to drink. She continued to advocate for better conditions for poor pregnant women and their new babies. The village had midwives, but inadequate medical care led to many deaths of mothers and babies. Until age seventy-five, Jerusha traveled to Bombay three times a week to see patients and to attend meetings.

In 1966 she was awarded the *Padma Shree*, the second highest distinction of India, by the Indian government for her work in obstetrics and gynecology and for her outstanding service in social welfare. She had been a pioneer in her thinking about women's health, both medical and social, speaking about the need for women to have fair pay, reasonable jobs, maternity leave, and daycare centers for their children. She believed in a solid education for women. She organized and encouraged work for the general welfare of mothers and children and for the blind and the physically disabled. She also helped establish feeding centers, rescue homes and children's aid societies.

One day as she and her sister sat together at home in Dahisar awaiting their morning coffee, Leah died. After her sister's death, Jerusha's own health began to fail and her eyesight grew dim. She continued to give away her money and belongings to those who were needy.

On June 2, 1984 at age ninety-three, Dr. Jerusha J. Jhirad died in Dahisar, maintaining until the end her belief that, "It is our duty to help others live in dignity."

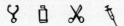

# 6

# Dr. Lucille Teasdale

1929    1996

BY THE TIME DR. LUCILLE TEASDALE died of AIDS, she weighed little more than seventy pounds.

Lucille had always been a rebel, fighting for what was right and just. Even as a girl she would speak her mind to the Catholic nuns who were her teachers. When she was twelve, missionaries told her class about the baby girls in China who were abandoned by their parents because girls were considered worthless. Lucille was outraged at this injustice. When the missionaries led the class in a Chinese prayer, Lucille, fascinated by the strangeness of a different culture, decided to become a doctor in Asia.

Her family was poor and lived in the east end of Montreal, near the docks. She and her four sisters slept in one room, her parents in another and her two brothers in the living room. Her mother suffered from depression, which often created a sad and difficult atmosphere in the house. Lucille was the fourth child, strong-willed and very smart. Her father was delighted when she told him of her plan to become a doctor. He was a butcher who wanted his children to better themselves through education.

In 1955, Lucille earned her MD with honors from the Université de Montréal. She became the first female surgeon in Quebec, and one of the first in Canada.

While she was studying surgery, she met an Italian doctor who had come to Canada to learn pediatrics (medicine of childhood) and radiology (x-rays). Dr. Piero Corti, four years older than Lucille, was the fifth of ten children from a wealthy family. He had a keen interest in motorcycles and sports cars — and, it turned out, in Lucille.

Because she wanted to go to the United States to learn to perform surgery on children, Lucille worked twice as many nights and performed twice as many operations as the male surgery residents. But even with glowing letters of recommendation, all twenty American universities to which she applied turned her down. In 1960, a woman surgeon was still an oddity in North America. As second choice, Lucille applied to two hospitals in France. Both accepted her, and soon she was off to Marseilles to study surgical pediatrics.

Meanwhile, Piero Corti had visited his brother, a Jesuit missionary in Africa. Deeply touched by the people's

> "Everyone tried to discourage me [from becoming a surgeon] by saying that no mother would ever put her child's life into the hands of a woman surgeon. In those days [the 1950s] you accepted that women weren't allowed to do certain things."
> – Lucille Teasdale

desperate need for medical care, Piero decided he would move to a small mission hospital near Gulu in northern Uganda, just above the equator in East Africa. The hospital was called St. Mary's Lacor.

When Lucille arrived in France she contacted Piero in Italy, where he was making plans to leave for Uganda. He asked that she come with him as a surgeon, just for a few months. After some hesitation she agreed. In May 1961, they arrived in Gulu with a few pieces of medical equipment, some medicines and money donated by Piero's relatives and friends.

St. Mary's Lacor Hospital had forty beds, one nurse, no doctor and a small chapel. Yet this tiny clinic served half a million people! At that time men in the area rarely lived past age forty, or women past forty-four. The simplest illness could cause death.

From the outset Lucille was intrigued by the beliefs and customs of the Acoli (pronounced Acholi) people, who lived in the Gulu area. Soon she realized that parents were having the roots of their children's canine teeth — the sharp, pointed teeth near the front of the mouth — removed by local healers, who often used an old bicycle spoke. Many

children died of infection or other complications. Lucille and
Piero came to understand that canine teeth were thought of
as "evil" teeth. The Acoli people believed that if those teeth
were allowed to grow in, the cattle would die and the rains
would not come. Lucille and Piero tried to explain to the parents the connection between this custom and the deaths of
their children, but with limited success.

Lucille remembered her childhood dream of doctoring
in Asia, and imagined St. Mary's growing into a large modern hospital with a surgical unit and African doctors.
However, her plan had been to return to France to pursue
her studies. The night before she was to leave, Piero asked
her to marry him and to share his new life in Gulu. They
married on December 5, 1961, surrounded by nuns in the
hospital chapel.

**Lucille and Piero, many years after they were married.**

Lucille and Piero began to raise money in Italy and
Canada so they could add to the hospital. Soon there was a
women's ward, a men's ward, a children's ward, an x-ray
department, a special section for people with malnutrition,
an isolation section for those with contagious diseases and
an operating room. Lucille was the surgeon and doctor for
outpatients over age six. She also taught the Italian doctors

who came for training. Piero was the pediatrician, radiologist, anesthesiologist (the doctor who keeps patients from feeling pain during surgery by using certain drugs) and medical director. Every morning they were up at seven o'clock. Lucille had her coffee and toast (with Quebec maple syrup) while listening to the news from Britain on her radio. Then she put on her white lab coat and walked down the hill to the hospital.

On a Saturday night in 1962, their only child, Dominique, was born. The next day Lucille rested. On Monday, she performed surgery. She had seen that the Acoli women went back to work within hours of giving birth, and she wanted to be as strong as her African friends and patients.

Sometimes Dominique felt ignored by her busy parents, but she played with her friends in the hospital compound. When Dominique was almost ten years old, Lucille and Piero made a painful decision — they would send their beloved daughter to live in Italy with Piero's relatives.

Dominique was angry and hurt, but she understood that it would be dangerous to remain in Gulu. A young military officer named Idi Amin Dada had become dictator of Uganda in 1971. Under his dictatorship tribal wars began. The Nilotic people of the north, supported by Amin, were killing the Bantu people of the south, who were supported by the British. Amin encouraged the Nilotics to completely wipe out Bantu groups such as the Acoli. Lucille and Piero feared that Amin's soldiers would come to Gulu. Dominique had to be protected, but they themselves needed to stay at the hospital.

Three years later Dominique left Italy to attend a boarding school in Kenya, an African country near Uganda. A group of nuns from Montreal paid her tuition, because her parents had little money. During her school vacations Dominique came home to Gulu. Sometimes she and her father went on safari.

In 1979, civil war began in Uganda. Amin's troops were defeated by an army from nearby Tanzania, but hundreds of thousands of innocent people were killed. Many soldiers loyal to Dictator Amin retreated to Gulu. Every night these soldiers — some of whom were very young — would rob and kill. One night, twelve cars filled with Amin's supporters broke into the hospital compound, firing their automatic weapons and looting the buildings. They beat up Piero, threatening to shoot him, but instead they disappeared with the hospital's vehicles.

The Lucille Teasdale and Piero Corti Foundation, created by two of Lucille's sisters, is a charity run by Piero and Dominique to raise money for St. Mary's Lacor Hospital and to promote their example of humanitarian care.

Both soldiers and ordinary citizens were brought to St. Mary's during the night with spear, arrow or soft-bullet wounds. Soft bullets shatter the victim's bones into splinters as sharp as glass. Many times, Lucille would cut herself on the bone fragments as she tried to dig out the bullets with her thumb and forefinger. She wore surgical gloves, but to save money for the hospital she sterilized the gloves and re-used them. They eventually wore out and ripped.

In this war zone Lucille and Piero worked day and night. For many years they had begged Ugandan officials to send medical interns from the nearest university to be trained at the hospital — their plan had been to make St.

Mary's a truly African hospital with all African staff. But medical residents did not want to come to a place of killing. Finally, in 1983, an African named Matthew Lukwiya came to work with Lucille and Piero. Everyone loved Dr. Lukwiya. He was compassionate and hard-working as well as devoted to his patients and to Lucille and Piero, with whom he worked as a team. Dr. Lukwiya alerted the world to Uganda's first Ebola virus outbreak. He taught citizens to recognize the symptoms of this vicious virus and made hospital staff understand how important it was to wear protective clothing when treating Ebola patients.

During the 1970s, Lucille, Piero and their growing staff started a school of nursing that trained hundreds of Ugandan healthcare professionals. In the 1980s, Lucille started a training program for Ugandan doctors who wanted to become surgeons.

Then personal tragedy struck. In 1985 Lucille tested positive for HIV, the virus that leads to AIDS. During the war, when she had been cut repeatedly by bone fragments during surgery, patients' infected blood had got into her cuts. At the time no one knew much about AIDS. But by the mid-1980s the disease was spreading quickly throughout Uganda and many parts of Africa. Lucille continued to work in her usual disciplined and dignified way, even though she had been told she would be dead within two years.

She became sicker, but insisted on keeping up a hectic pace. In 1986, during more fighting, the hospital was repeatedly looted and some staff kidnapped. On Good Friday, 1989, Dr. Lukwiya and five nurses were dragged into the bush and forced to treat wounded soldiers. They were released one week later, alive but terrified.

As fighting grew more intense, villagers whose homes had been destroyed came flooding into the hospital compound for protection, food and medical care. Ten thousand people hid there every night! The hospital compound had become a makeshift refugee camp.

By the early 1990s, Lucille was performing only the most difficult operations. She was also in charge of the new sixty-bed tuberculosis (TB) ward, where 60% of the patients were HIV positive. Dr. Lukwiya and Piero also worked tirelessly. They started a new outpatient department and an intensive care unit for very sick patients. St. Mary's became the second largest hospital in Uganda, with 400 staff members. Being in the heart of the civil war zone, it was filled every day with children and adults whose limbs had been blown off by land mines, or whose homes had been destroyed and families murdered. There was no family in Gulu untouched by AIDS.

> Lucille was appointed a Member of the Order of Canada (1991) and a laureate of the Canadian Medical Hall of Fame (2001). A Canadian stamp was issued in her name in 2000, and there is a permanent exhibition of her life story at Ottawa's Canada And The World Pavilion.

Children were also dying of malaria, pneumonia, malnutrition, measles and diarrhea. More and more babies and children were orphaned because of AIDS. So Lucille kept working. She remained brave — saving people's lives gave her a reason to live. So did Dominique, her pride and joy. Dominique graduated from the University of Milan medical school in 1995, and married an Italian doctor just as her mother had.

Eleven years after being diagnosed with AIDS, Lucille was too ill to go on working. She traveled to Italy in April

1996, where she died a few months later at the age of sixty-seven. Piero had comforted her in those last days by reminding her that Dr. Lukwiya, their friend and colleague, was keeping the hospital running. She could go peacefully, knowing that Piero had a partner to help him continue their work.

A memorial procession and service were held in Piero's home town of Besana, Italy, but Lucille wanted to be buried on the grounds of St. Mary's Lacor Hospital, under a frangipani plant. In the thirty-five years she had been at St. Mary's, Lucille had performed more than 13,000 operations.

In the year 2000 the Ebola virus returned to Uganda. Dr. Lukwiya, then forty-three years old and a father of five, notified the health authorities. Two months later he died, having been infected by a patient. His dying wish was to be buried next to his mentor and friend, Dr. Lucille. The hospital staff and patients were crushed by the loss.

Today Piero remains co-ordinator of St. Mary's, but the staff is entirely African. The hospital has 463 beds and often handles 600 patients — usually with two children in each bed. Because civil war continues, every day at least eight major operations take place, mainly for wounds from weapons or land mines. TB is still another major cause of death.

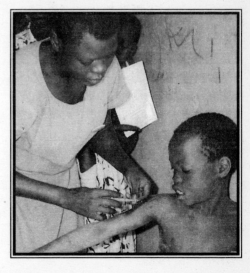

Thousands of people continue to sleep in the hospital compound to escape the war. They now have a semipermanent shelter. The staff at St. Mary's also built and run an orphanage. The children who stay there were born with HIV or were orphaned by AIDS or war. Some have been badly injured by land mines that they stepped on by accident. The orphanage also treats children suffering from malnutrition, malaria, pneumonia or measles.

The tiny clinic Lucille and Piero arrived at in May 1961 has grown into a modern healthcare facility, a beacon of hope for people who have known only hunger and the terrors of war and disease. It was the lifelong vision of a woman who began her fight for justice as a rebellious schoolgirl in Montreal. In her humble, no-nonsense yet passionate way, Lucille Teasdale brought courage and her surgical skills to improve the health of thousands of people who loved her.

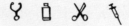

# 7

# Dr. Joy Seager

1899          1991

Joy Debenham Seager had a pet kangaroo named Kanga, which loved to sit on Joy's lap when she was talking on the telephone. When Kanga was a baby, Joy nailed a tea cosy (a knitted teapot cover) to the back of a door as a pouch for her to sleep in. At first Kanga ate from an eyedropper; later Joy taught her to lap milk from a saucer like a cat. At night she slept outside, but during the day she played with the dogs and cats. The cats would lick the milk right off Kanga's mouth.

Kanga's other companions included two swans, a possum, a magpie named Quirk, two peacocks, a wild duck, two kookaburras and more than a thousand sheep. There were also fleas everywhere! Joy, her husband and her children referred to their home as "Seager Circus."

Joy moved from England to Sydney, Australia with her parents and two older sisters when she was ten years old, because her father had taken a job as Superintendent of Music for the state of New South Wales. Joy settled into school, played field hockey and tennis and learned lifesaving skills as a swimmer. She was a strong student and won a scholarship to the University of Sydney. In Joy's medical school class there were twenty-five women; the rest were men. In 1924 she graduated as a doctor. Her family was very proud to have another doctor in the family — Joy's grandfather and great-uncle had also been physicians.

Now she had to find a job. She applied to the Balmain Hospital, and although they were impressed with her record and her excellent letters of reference, they would not accept her as a resident (an apprentice doctor) because there was no bathroom for a woman. What an excuse! Instead, Joy took a job as assistant to a resident at the Royal Alexandra Children's Hospital, where there were already two senior women residents.

Just at that time, in the 1920s, there was an outbreak of diphtheria among children. Diphtheria is a deadly disease in which the victim chokes to death. Today babies are protected against diphtheria, whooping cough, and tetanus by a vaccine, but back then babies were not automatically immunized. Joy worked very hard fighting diphtheria and other diseases at the hospital, but received no pay.

Her next job was as the very first resident at a clinic run

by and for women. At the beginning doctors were available evenings only, and Joy earned just enough to pay for her streetcar fare to and from work. Today that clinic has become one of Sydney's largest hospitals, the Rachel Forster Hospital.

Later that year, Joy was appointed Medical Superintendent at St. John's Church of England Hospital, in the town of Young. There she could use her skills as a midwife (someone who helps mothers deliver their babies) because most of her patients were pregnant women. It was while she was in Young that she heard that a doctor was urgently needed on Kangaroo Island.

> Kangaroo Island is off the south coast of Australia. It is a tiny place, only 145 kilometers long, and 55 kilometers at its widest. Today it is a tourist para- dise with bays, beaches, high cliffs and a raging sea on the south. It is warm in winter and cool in summer, and fish are abundant. However, when early settlers cleared the land, they found that the soil was too poor to grow crops.

When Joy arrived on the island she was twenty-six years old. She was alone, did not know any of the Islanders, and was the only doctor. Quickly, she learned two things: first, that most of the inhabitants were very poor, and sec- ond, that most of the people on the island came from just a few families, each with legions of children. It was not unusual for people to have sixteen children — one man had twenty-four, although he might have had them with more than one wife. Imagine naming all those babies! Once, a clergyman was christening twins named Kate and Sydney. He got so confused he said, "I now name these children Steak and Kidney." After a few years on Kangaroo Island, Joy realized that many new baby girls were being named "Joy."

When she first arrived she lived in the small capital town of Kingscote, where she rented the front half of a house and used one of the rooms as her office. The Islanders were grateful to have a doctor, especially one who was willing to travel long distances on horseback, often along narrow tracks through dense bush. Sometimes she traveled at night, listening for the sounds of kangaroos, wallabies, possums, wild pigs and tiger snakes.

The only telephones on Kangaroo Island were at post offices and lighthouses. If anybody fell ill, someone would have to make the long trip to a telephone to call the post office in Kingscote. A person there would describe the problem to Joy, and she would gallop off to see her patient. Sometimes by the time she got there the patient had died or the baby had been born. Then she would do whatever was necessary.

At first, tuberculosis (TB) seemed to be everywhere. Joy taught the Islanders about keeping themselves clean and preparing food properly. She also began doing regular physical examinations so that she could catch problems when they were still small, and she sent patients to the mainland for x-rays if she thought they had TB. Soon her efforts paid off — there were no more cases of tuberculosis on the Island!

Conditions remained very primitive. There was no dentist, so Joy became the tooth puller. There was no surgeon to perform operations. No child had ever received a vaccination against diphtheria and tetanus, and many children died of these diseases.

Joy convinced the Board of Health to supply her with the serum to inoculate every child on the Island. First she went to all the schools, then to all the outback farms where children did their lessons at home. In the outback the land is flat and dry, and farms are far apart. Joy bought a car, so she could bump along the roads and pathways to the center of the island. No matter how rough the ride, she always arrived in good humor.

**Joy locks up her doctor's office, a shed behind a gas station.**

A young man Joy had met began to visit her often, and after some time he asked her to marry him. His name was Hal Seager, and he and his brother Ted lived on a sheep farm they called Hawk's Nest. It was only forty-two kilometers from Kingscote, but because of the bad roads it took two-and-a-half hours to get there from town. Joy was tempted to marry Hal, but she had three more years on her contract as the Kangaroo Island doctor. The Island Council decided that if she agreed to come into town to her office twice a week, and to attend to every patient who called her out when they needed medical attention, she did not have to live in Kingscote. Joy accepted their terms — and Hal's offer of marriage — and moved out to Hawk's Nest.

Hal's brother Ted and his new wife lived on the farm, too, but in their own house. Joy had a telephone installed so that she could be reached through the post office. She moved her office to a room in the local pub and hotel. But because her "waiting room" was the wide porch of the hotel, everyone who strolled along the main street could see who was visiting the doctor that day. There was absolutely no privacy. Another difficulty was that when the pub owner drank too much, he would follow Joy around asking, "What's the matter with that one, doc?"

That was the last straw. Joy moved the office again, to a shed situated behind a gas station. Unfortunately the shed was not soundproof, and on Saturday mornings children would gather around behind it with their ears to the wall. Listening to what was going on in the office was the best free entertainment of the week.

The world-wide Great Depression that started in 1929 left most people even poorer than they had been before. Hal and Joy had money to buy tea and sugar, but not much else. They grew their own wheat, vegetables, apricots, winter peas, almonds and walnuts. They had hives for honey and meat from sheep. Joy's patients were poor, too, so they paid her with food from their farms, or a family member would do jobs on Joy's farm such as helping to dig a well.

Even though Joy and Hal laughed a lot together and had fun with Ted and his wife, farming was physically demanding. They were up before sunrise. Hal and Ted would have the workhorses fed and harnessed before breakfast, after having already drawn twenty-four buckets of water from the well. At least twice a week Joy drove into Kingscote, two-and-a-half hours each way. On the other days — and nights — she might be called all over the island to deal with medical emergencies.

A common call was from people who had been bitten by the poisonous tiger snakes that slithered through the bush and into houses. Joy would make a cut where the snake fangs had entered and suck the wound, spitting out the blood. If necessary, she would give an injection to prevent infection.

Once a man cut his leg with an axe. Joy had been away from the house when someone came to find her. She did not want to waste time going home for her doctor's bag, and therefore had no painkillers, no thread to sew up the cut and no dressing for the wound. Calmly, she asked someone in the house to sterilize a sewing needle in the fire while she went outside to take a look at their horse. She selected six long hairs from the horse's tail and went back indoors where she threaded the needle with the first horse hair and made a stitch in the big, ugly wound. She kept stitching until the cut was completely closed, and then ripped up a sheet for a dressing to put over the wound. Weeks later, she returned to remove the horsehair stitches and found her patient completely recovered.

Joy's hospital was for everyone – both white people and Aborigines. Some white people disagreed with this policy, but Joy stood her ground. She insisted that a general practitioner be "a friend to all his or her patients" – and the feeling would be mutual.

After almost twenty years on what Joy and Hal called their "island of dreams," she was becoming exhausted. She seemed never to stop working. Then the Director-General of

Medical Services in Australia wrote, asking whether she would consider moving to Kingston, on the mainland. The people needed a doctor there because of a diphtheria epidemic. One child had already died and they feared many more would follow. Joy and Hal agreed to move, in part because their son, Michael, and daughter, Genevieve, were ready for high school, and there was none in Kingscote.

Tearfully, the Islanders bid them farewell. In 1945, the family settled into Kingston with its sea breezes and beaches. The children went to school, and Joy was not only the doctor, but also the local veterinarian. The town had no ambulance to send people to the hospital in the city of Adelaide, and no pharmacist to prepare medications. Joy counted out the pills or measured the powders and potions, Hal wrote the labels, and Genevieve and Michael wrapped the bottles in clean white paper and placed a drop of sealing wax on each to keep it secure.

Joy rented a four-room house and turned it into a hospital. She begged her friends to help by working as "nurses," but conditions in the hospital were so unpleasant that her friends usually did not stay long.

Once Joy brought in a surgeon from the city to operate on all the children who needed their tonsils removed. She called it a "tonsil event." She also responded to a polio epidemic in South Australia, which left many people handicapped for life. But mainly she dealt with the delivery of babies, snakebites, school accidents, bronchitis and allergies.

In the early 1950s, after six years in Kingston, Joy found that she was developing arthritis in her back. She sold her medical practice and the family moved to a farm in nearby Mount Pleasant. They sent for some of the sheep from their old farm at Hawk's Nest. Money was scarce, however, so Joy took a job as a school doctor. Michael, aged sixteen, left school to help his father on the farm because Hal's eyesight was failing. In 1964, Joy turned sixty-five, so she had to retire from the School Health Department.

For the next five years she served as an eye doctor at the Royal Adelaide Hospital. Then at age seventy, she began a new job in a psychiatric ward for elderly patients.

Sadly, Hal's eyesight kept getting worse, and for his last few years he was completely blind. In January 1976, he died at age eighty-six. Joy, then in her late seventies, returned to work, but it was no longer satisfying. With Hal's death she had lost her best friend.

She decided to go to university to work toward a Bachelor of Arts (BA) degree, but just as she was about to start her second course she received a phone call from an old friend named Stan. He told her that a cargo ship was sailing for England and needed a doctor on board. Would she be interested? Joy hesitated, but Michael encouraged her to take the leap into her next adventure. On board she discovered an active case of tuberculosis, and ensured it did not spread to the rest of the crew. She also discovered that Stan was in love with her. A year later, they married in a country church in South Australia. His son was the best man and her grandchildren were bridesmaids and flower girls. Genevieve arranged the reception, then Joy and Stan drove 100 kilometers to Stan's farm, where they lived happily.

Joy died in 1991. Today, Michael and his son farm the land in Mount Pleasant, where Michael, as a boy, had helped his father.

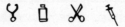

# 8

# Dr. Fe del Mundo

1911

A NOTE WRITTEN BY A GIRL IN GRADE THREE told of her plan to become a doctor who would cure the poor. But she would never carry out that plan, for she died soon after writing the note. Instead, her sister Fe would become that doctor.

Four of the eight children in Fe's family died, three of them as babies. Losing children to illness was not unusual in the Philippines. Fe del Mundo grew up there, in Old

Manila, a seaport on the South China Sea.

Fe's mother, Paz Villanueva, was up with the sun and off to the market to find food for her children. Besides taking care of the house, she ran a small bakery to give her family as many opportunities as she could. Fe's father, Bernardo del Mundo, was a prominent lawyer involved in local politics; yet his family lived in poverty because he was not a good businessman. He valued education and insisted that his children attend government schools, as those schools had high standards of teaching.

At home, discipline was strict: the children were to study hard, respect and obey their elders, and be seen and not heard when adults were present. Anyone who broke the rules was spanked. Fe was quiet and shy, anxious to please adults and very attached to her mother.

Shortly after Fe graduated from high school, her mother became very ill. Before she died, Paz asked her sister, Mercedes, to take care of her family and to give special attention to Fe. She was afraid that her daughter would be unable to cope without her. Although grief-stricken, Fe was determined to fulfil her sister's dream and to study medicine.

She won scholarships to the University of the Philippines at age fifteen. There she enjoyed math, physics and English, but was still so shy that sometimes she would cry when the teacher asked her to speak in class. After two years at university came the competition to win a spot in medical school. Tiny, determined Fe scored the highest mark on the entrance exam.

In medical school she faced long days of study, made more stressful by her poverty. Often she had no money for textbooks and had to borrow them from her classmates. In her fifth year, she almost dropped out of school because she could not pay the fee for writing her final exams. Her Aunt

Mercedes paid the fee for her, and Fe graduated with the highest marks in her class. She was awarded a medal for the Most Outstanding Scholar in Medicine for 1933. Then she took the national exam and ranked third in the whole country!

As part of her training, Fe had traveled into the countryside with a rural physician who diagnosed every childhood illness as "worms" (a parasite that lodges in the intestine and keeps the victim from receiving the nutrients in their food) and gave the same treatment for every symptom. Not surprisingly, many children died because doctors knew so little about childhood diseases. Fe decided that she would devote herself to pediatrics, the medical needs of children from before birth to adolescence. She would not only cure sick children, she would teach families how to live healthy lives and prevent illness. This would not be easy in a country where the greatest problem was malnutrition, and so many people lacked healthful food. But her name, Fe del Mundo, means "faith of the world," and she had faith both in God and in people.

> The Republic of the Philippines consists of a group of 7,100 islands in the Pacific Ocean, off the southeast coast of China. The first woman from the Philippines to graduate with an MD was Dr. Honorie Sison, in 1903.

Someone must have had faith in Fe, too. One evening a phone call informed her that the president of the Philippines, Manuel L. Quezon, was offering her a scholarship. She was instructed to appear at the palace the next morning, where she was granted money that would allow her to study pediatrics in the United States. It was her dream come true.

She went to Harvard Medical School in 1936. When she arrived in Boston and found her room, she realized that the university housing was for male students only. Harvard had never allowed a female to study at their medical school — they had thought that Fe was a man's name. But the head of Pediatrics saw that Fe's medical school record was too good to deny her entrance. She became the very first woman to attend Harvard Medical School. In her five years there, she not only finished her pediatric studies, but completed a master's degree in bacteriology, as well.

In 1941, all Filipinos studying abroad were called home because of the threat of World War II spreading to their country. On December 8, 1941, Japanese planes attacked the Philippines. (This was one day after the Japanese attack on the American naval base at Pearl Harbor, Hawaii.) Japanese troops invaded the Philippines, destroying much of the country as they took it over. The Philippine people were captives in their own land. But they were not alone; Americans, British and other foreigners whose countries were at war with Japan were locked in an internment camp, a makeshift prison situated on the campus of the University of Santo Tomas.

In January 1942, with help from the Red Cross, Fe organized a special home for the 400 children — aged five months to fourteen years old — who had been sent to the

> Fe has written more than 100 articles for medical journals, and had a weekly column in *The Manila Sunday Times Magazine* for twenty years. She also organized the Philippine Medical Women's Association, helped create the Philippine Pediatric Society, and taught in two medical schools.

internment camp with their parents. The Japanese allowed them to live in the children's home, and Fe gave them medical care. She even arranged drives to nearby parks so they could play. In 1944, all the children were forced back to the internment camp.

Fe kept working for children. She set up a hospital in a school to provide medical care for Filipino children living with the terror of war. When the Japanese surrendered on September 2, 1945, Fe's children's hospital became available for all people who had suffered injuries, and Fe became the first woman to run a public hospital. There she established a school of nursing.

Some of the many honors given to Fe:
She was the first Philippine national to be certified by the American Board of Pediatrics as Board Diplomat.
She was the first Asian elected president of the Medical Women's International Association.
She received honorary doctorates in science from Medical Women's College in Pennsylvania and Smith College (USA).
She received the Most Distinguished Pediatrician and Humanitarian Award from the International Pediatric Association (1977), and the Ramon Magsaysay Award for public service given by a private citizen (also 1977).

After the war, there was so much to do to rebuild her ravaged country. She continued to work ceaselessly to improve children's lives. Many mothers begged her not to send their sick children to hospital. They wanted Fe to look after them herself. And she did! She turned her house into the "Little Clinic," and before long she had no empty bed to sleep in herself. She searched the neighborhood for more space for sick children. Then Fe borrowed money to build a hospital in Manila, the capital city. The Children's Memorial Hospital, dedicated to the children of the Philippines, had 100 beds. In order to buy equipment, Fe sold her house and moved into the hospital.

She wanted to build a center for research into childhood health and illness, provide education and services for the prevention of diseases and hire staff who would travel to rural areas where living conditions were hazardous. And she did it all — the Institute of Maternal and Child Health (IMCH) opened in November 1972.

Bringing medical treatment to poor remote areas was especially important to Fe, because too many babies and children died before they had a chance to live. In the 1960s, she organized teams of doctors and other healthcare providers to teach local healthcare workers how to treat diarrhea and other diseases that threaten the lives of poor children, how to test the water supply for contamination and how to protect children against polio and other diseases.

Fe's Institute of Community and Family Health (ICFH) opened in 1973, focusing on the care of teenagers and on teaching villagers in remote areas how to take care of their own health.

Throughout the years, Fe started her day with a visit to church, to receive the spiritual strength she needed to get through her long days. She got up at five in the morning and went to sleep at midnight. For several years she lived in the Children's Hospital, sleeping in any room that was empty. Finally, she settled into a small suite on the fourth floor of the Institute of Maternal and Child Health, living on black coffee and hospital soup, and always working.

In 1976, her ideas were published in the *Textbook of Pediatrics and Child Health.* The book explained that the efforts of the whole community are required in order to bring good health to its children. The book also stated that children need to be fit in both body and spirit. Medical students learned that they should actually visit poor rural areas to experience the people's problems first-hand. Fe also urged doctors to speak in a way that patients understand when teaching about cleanliness, healthful food and how to control the number of children parents have.

On November 27, 2000, the Children's Medical Center changed its name to the Dr. Fe del Mundo Medical Center, to honor the woman who believes, "Give to the world the best you have and the best will come back to you." Dr. del Mundo is still going strong, even as she reaches the age of ninety.

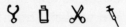

## 9

# Dr. Carolle Jean-Murat

**1950**

**Dr. Carolle with a young friend.**

IT WAS PITCH BLACK OUT when a loud knock woke eleven-year-old Carolle and her mother, Lamercie. A voice called out anxiously that one of the village women was about to give birth; alone, frightened and in pain, the pregnant woman needed Lamercie's help. People always called for her when there was an emergency. Lamercie's father was a Voodoo priest and a medicine man, from whom she had learned a lot about healing.

Carolle begged to go along, and soon they were rushing through the hot Caribbean night. She watched in amazement as her mother helped the woman give birth. Carolle felt proud — especially when Lamercie handed her the newborn to hold while she took care of the mother. One day, Carolle thought, she too would help bring babies into the world.

It was unusual for her to be staying with Lamercie, for she rarely saw her mother. At age four, Carolle and her two-year-old sister, Marise, had been sent to live with their grandmother in Port-au-Prince, the capital city of Haiti. Carolle's father, Joseph Karl Jean, had left the marriage, and Lamercie was very poor. No one in Lamercie's family had ever finished primary school, but in Joseph's family there were lawyers, teachers and judges. Joseph's father had been a pharmacist.

Lamercie knew that with Joseph's family, her children would have many more opportunities for a decent life than if they lived with her. It was very painful, but she gave her children to Joseph's mother, who lived with her unmarried daughter, Julia. Aunt Julia wanted Carolle and Marise to have nothing to do with Lamercie, believing her to be a bad influence. Whenever Carolle did see her mother, Lamercie cried with the misery of having to part again. Carolle promised herself that she would never be poor and uneducated like Lamercie, and vowed that one day she would be important and rich enough to look after Lamercie and her family.

Life was not easy for Carolle. Most of Haiti was, and still is, poverty-stricken. During Carolle's childhood the government was a dictatorship. People were kidnapped and killed if they were thought to be communists. One of those people was Carolle's uncle, who disappeared without a trace. Often books were burned if the government disagreed with the contents, so it was rare to find a book of any kind. A family friend who had a secret library in his house allowed Carolle to borrow his books. He saw how respectfully she treated them and how she longed to learn. Late into the night, she would read by candlelight. She was determined to make a difference in the world, to be "a champion of hope." Her Grandma taught her that all things are possible, that she could "go as far as any man could ever go." This attitude was extraordinary, because higher education was for a few lucky boys only.

When Carolle was nine she became very ill. Her Grandma took her from doctor to doctor, but she did not get better. Finally, Lamercie learned of her child's sickness, and insisted that Carolle be taken to her father, Mirabeau Murat, the Voodoo healer. Carolle imagined this unknown grandfather would be a scary demon, but when they met she saw that he was a kind and loving man. He treated her, and her illness disap-

> In Haiti, 75% of the population lives in poverty, without access to enough food, safe drinking water, or medical care; 60% are unemployed, and 55% are illiterate (they cannot read or write).

peared. When she was well again, she told Grandfather Mirabeau that someday she would become a healer also. She thought he would be pleased, but he was not. He told her that Lamercie had made a great sacrifice in sending her children away to give them a brighter future. If Carolle became a Voodoo healer, he said, that sacrifice would have been wasted. Study hard, he advised her, and become a medical doctor. Then he would be very proud.

Although Carolle was angry with her father for leaving her mother, she loved him deeply. Joseph's work took him away much of the time, but when he was at home, he was supportive and caring. Like Grandma, he would remind his daughters that they could pursue any dream they wished. The hard labor that caused the calluses on his hands was his way of ensuring they would have the money to follow those dreams.

St. Joseph's Hospital in Haiti

Sometimes Joseph did not get paid for months, and then the family went hungry. Grandma would rub Carolle's empty belly, and together they would pray for a better tomorrow. They could have escaped poverty if Joseph had agreed to join the cruel *tontons macoutes*, the dictator's secret police, but he did not believe in using weapons. This was a dangerous belief in Haiti; when Carolle was fifteen years old, her father was kidnapped and tortured by the *tontons macoutes*. He would have been killed, but a childhood friend who had become a high-ranking secret police officer had him freed. Joseph knew it was only a matter of time before he would be killed, and had no choice but to leave Haiti. Eventually he made his way to New York, where he worked day and night until he was able to send for two of Carolle's younger sisters.

Throughout Carolle's complicated childhood, her Grandma was a source of comfort and inspiration. Although not educated, the older woman knew all the herbs by name and how to transform them into remedies for illnesses and into potions for maintaining good health. She had never heard of a woman doctor, yet thought it a fine idea that

Carolle become one.

When she was sixteen, Carolle got a summer job as an assistant to a nurse who ran a small medical clinic in a rural town. This experience inspired Carolle to pursue a medical career and, later, to build a hospital for the poor. She completed her pre-medicine studies at the university in Port-au-Prince, then studied medicine in Mexico and Jamaica. In 1978, she started four years of training in obstetrics and gynecology (the treatment of women and babies) in Milwaukee, Wisconsin. The United States was a real challenge: cold weather was a new experience for her. More significantly, some of her teachers discriminated against women and people of color. But Carolle drew herself up to her full six-foot height and let those doctors know that she planned to do outstanding things, and that if they gave her a good education, she would always remember them kindly. It worked: Carolle graduated as a specialist in obstetrics and gynecology. She had completed the journey begun that dark night in Haiti, when Lamercie helped the young mother to give birth. Now it was Carolle's turn.

In the early 1980s, Dr. Carolle settled in San Diego, California. For thirteen years she was the only Black female obstetrician-gynecologist in San Diego County. For four years she was the only female surgeon on staff at her hospital.

She believes that doctors have to treat the whole person, not just the symptoms. She pictures good health as being like a table, set on four legs: physical, mental, spiritual and financial health. She listens carefully and caringly to her patients, then together they choose the solution — surgery and/or other healing practices — that seems right for the patient. It is no surprise that Dr. Carolle combines old and new ideas; after all, her grandparents and mother had used home remedies, Voodoo healing, prayer, touch and caring. Before surgery, Dr. Carolle reassuringly holds her patient's hand until they drift off.

She provides free medical care to homeless women, and is director of the Southern Indian Health Council. She teaches at the School of Medicine at the University of California, San Diego. Because she is fluent in Haitian, French, Spanish, English and Italian, she can communicate easily with women of many different backgrounds.

For many years, Dr. Carolle could not return to her homeland. It was too dangerous because the Haitian government often saw people returning to Haiti as a threat. Finally, she decided to take the risk. She joined a team bringing medical care from America twice a year to La Vallée de Jacmel, a town high in the mountains, three hours from Port-au-Prince. Its thirty-bed hospital, St. Joseph's, is staffed with one medical intern, two nurses, one midwife and two nuns. This small group cares for the 100,000 people who live in the surrounding areas! Most sick people in Haiti die because they lack basic medical care, so Dr. Carolle "adopted" St. Joseph's. She works hard to convince people in wealthier countries to contribute money, medical supplies and their skills to support the hospital.

Near St. Joseph's is a high school, Lycée Philippe Jules, attended by about 750 poor children in La Vallée. Most of the students have to walk miles to get to school, and most of them are hungry. Yet they are eager to study, since education is their only ticket to a better life. Dr. Carolle tells them that sometimes she, too, went to bed hungry, but she herself escaped poverty through education. She and her team give scholarships to the top five students in each of the eight classes every year. They also give scholarships to 200 of the neediest children, and are searching for other sponsors — only $100 pays for one student's schooling for a whole year! Dr. Carolle and her team have raised money for a generator to provide the Lycée with electricity, and they are now buying computers to link the school to the rest of the world.

Dr. Carolle has written books (such as *Staying Healthy: 10 Easy Steps for Women*) and received several awards including the 1995 Outstanding Black Leader Award from Channel 8 (a CBS affiliate), the 1996 Catholic Charities Award for outstanding service to the Medical Screening Program, and the 1999 Woman of Excellence Award from the Beta Pi Sigma Society (a college club).

In 1993, she created a cable TV talk show called *Let's Stay Healthy,* a project of her non-profit organization called the Health Through Communications Foundation. She has recorded audiotapes and written articles for magazines and newspapers, and has made numerous television appearances promoting the importance of being informed about one's health. She also has a web site so people can ask her medical questions. One of her greatest gifts is the ability to explain medical information in a way that ordinary people can understand. She presents her ideas in a clear, caring and sometimes even funny way.

Dr. Carolle travels around the world to encourage women to take charge of their lives and their health. She says, "All things are possible if you believe in them. No obstacle is too large to overcome if you know what you want. Nothing can stop you from achieving your goals if you believe in them and work to attain them."

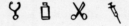

# Dr. Nadine Caron

**1970**

NADINE AND HER THREE BROTHERS grew up in Kamloops, British Columbia, Canada. Her mother, Mabel, had been raised on an Ojibway reserve in Northern Ontario. Her father, Zefferino, had emigrated from Italy to Canada. When they were young both Mabel and Zefferino rose above many obstacles, and as parents they taught through example the

importance of hard work, determination and self-confi-
dence. Their home was a bustling, loving place with
everyone working hard and playing hard.

In high school, Nadine acted in dramatic productions,
played basketball, soccer and volleyball and also ran track.
She loved to try everything! In 1988 she entered Simon
Fraser University in Burnaby, British Columbia with academic and basketball scholarships that continued for five
years. As her skills developed she began to seriously consider a career as a professional athlete, but there were no
women's professional basketball teams in Canada.

For three years (1989–1992), Nadine's university team
traveled to the National Women's Basketball Championships
in Jackson, Tennessee, USA. Their host was an organization
called the Hospital Corporation of America. Members
showed the players around the town and looked after their
every need. One year they asked the young women whether
any of them had an interest in becoming a doctor. Until that
time, Nadine had been working toward a degree in kinesiology, the study of human movement, which physical
education teachers must learn. She had studied anatomy,
physiology and biochemistry, but it had never occurred to
her to become a doctor. She knew that, although so many
paths excited her, some day she would have to choose one.

Nadine told her hosts in Jackson that she might consider a career in medicine because she enjoyed her courses
in kinesiology. Soon after, she spent the summer of 1992 in
a hospital in Jackson, shadowing a surgeon as he went
about his daily work. Nadine felt a special connection to
surgery, as though she had been meant for it. She was
hooked, and spent the next two summers in Jackson learning all she could.

Back she went for her fifth year at Simon Fraser
University to finish her degree in kinesiology (1993), and to

apply to medical school at the University of British Columbia (UBC) in Vancouver. Nadine had relished being a student at Simon Fraser — she liked being able to choose subjects she cared about, and the more interested she was, the higher her grades were.

No one in Nadine's family had ever been a doctor. She knew that medical school was a long and costly venture, one she could not afford. Because her university grades were high, UBC awarded her scholarships. Her mother's band, the Sagamok Anishnawbe, gave her additional money through their Sudbury Area Post-Secondary Counseling Unit.

Medical school opened up new avenues for Nadine, but she kept coming back to surgery. She understood that being a surgeon required dedication, commitment to six years of study beyond medical school, long working hours and lots of practice. After four years of medical school, Nadine received her MD in May 1997. Of the 120 graduates, she had the highest grades! On top of that, she was the first Native woman to graduate from UBC's faculty of medicine.

"I should have ripped my medical diploma in half," she says, "and given half of it to my parents. They have always been so supportive. They taught me to count my blessings and to believe in myself."

On July 1, 1997, Nadine began her residency in general surgery at UBC. After three years, she decided to take a year to pursue her interests in medical research and in health issues related to Native Canadians. She wanted to study government policies that, directly or indirectly, lead to major health problems among Native people. She applied to Harvard University and received a large scholarship from the National Aboriginal Achievement Foundation in Canada, plus awards from several other supportive organizations. After her year at Harvard she received her master's degree in public health (MPH) in June 2001.

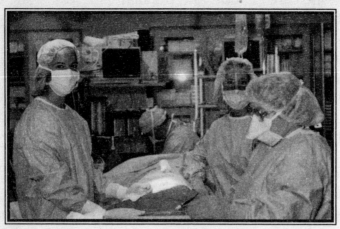

**Nadine (left) as a surgical resident in the operating room.**

While some medical students and residents might want to relax during their hard-earned vacation, Nadine has spent part of hers volunteering with the Scientists and Innovators in the Schools program, sponsored by Science World, Vancouver's museum of science. She travels throughout British Columbia speaking to children from kindergarten to grade twelve. She shares her delight in science and nature, sometimes using a cow's heart to explain the circulatory system to students, or showing them a human heart that has suffered a heart attack, or how a blood-pressure cuff works. Whatever she chooses to discuss, her audience clearly sees that Nadine loves the topic. Sometimes she does not talk about medicine at all; instead, she demonstrates her basketball or soccer skills by playing with the children.

She prefers to travel to remote areas of the province,

where young people are less likely to have as many oppor-tunities as those in bigger towns and cities. Nadine wants them to understand that, even though university might seem like an impossible dream, education is the stepping stone to their future. She tells them that they must believe in themselves, even if they face roadblocks. She reminds them that money is available through community organiza-tions to help students continue their education.

Nadine has been involved with the British Columbia Medical Association Committee on Aboriginal Health and is a member of the Native Physicians Association of Canada. There are still very few Native doctors — only about 200 in all of Canada.

She also believes in the right balance between hard work and fun, and rarely sits still. Nadine competes in triathlons, complet-ing a two-kilometer swim and fifty-five-kilometer bike ride before finishing with an exhaust-ing fifteen-kilometer run. At other times she plays basketball and soccer.

Two years remain of Nadine's six-year surgery residency. After that she might continue as a resident for another two years, to specialize in a certain type of surgery. By then, she will have been studying to be a doctor for twelve years! Still, Nadine views this schooling as a privilege, not as a burden. She has not let all her scholarships and awards, her athletic abilities or popularity in the schools distract her from her goals. She remains focused on the medical work she can do among Native people and other Canadians. With time and talent on her side, she can look forward to achieving many important "firsts."

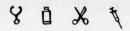

# ☆ Glossary ☆
## of Medical Terms

**AIDS** — acquired immunodeficiency syndrome, first reported in 1981; caused by the human immunodeficiency virus (HIV), which attacks the immune system, leaving the person open to serious illnesses that can cause death.

**allergies** — oversensitivity to certain substances, causing the immune system to respond to the substance. If one parent is allergic, then a child has a one-in-four chance of developing an allergy, but they might be allergic to different things.

**anesthesia** — a drug or gas used before surgery to block out the patient's awareness of pain; anesthesiologist — a physician who gives anesthesia and then monitors the patient's need for more or less of it during surgery.

**anatomy** — the science of the structure of animals or plants.

**antibiotics** — chemicals used as drugs to kill or slow the growth of microorganisms. The drugs treat bacterial infections, but do not work on infections caused by viruses.

**arthritis** — an inflammation that leads to pain and swelling in the joints. Very common.

**bacteria** — one-celled organisms which can be seen only with a microscope. Some cause diseases but others are necessary for survival.

**bronchitis** — inflammation of the lungs' air passages, usually from an infection or chemical irritation. Coughing and spitting occur.

**cholera** — a severe infectious intestinal disease characterized by extreme diarrhea, intestinal pain, and dehydration (loss of body fluids).

**contagious disease** — one that is easily spread.

**diarrhea** — inflammation or irritation of the intestines, usually from an infection. Can cause death because of severe dehydration (loss of body fluids).

**diphtheria** — a highly contagious childhood disease that affects the throat; in bad cases, a membrane and swelling can develop in the throat, causing severe breathing problems.

**dissect** — to cut apart piece by piece, such as when medical students cut apart a dead body for the purpose of study.

**dysentery** — intestinal inflammation with abdominal pain and intense diarrhea.

**Ebola virus** — a virus discovered in 1976, and named after a river in Zaire, Africa, where it was first detected. The natural host of the virus remains unknown. Can cause fever, headaches, muscle aches, vomiting, diarrhea, sore throat, chest pain, and in some cases, internal bleeding leading to death.

**epidemic** — the quick spread of a disease throughout a population. For example, in 1918, an influenza epidemic killed 20 million people as it spread from France throughout the world.

**geriatrics** — the care and medical problems of older people.

**gynecologist** — a physician who specializes in the health and diseases of female reproductive organs.

**herbs** — a plant used as medicine, food, and/or certain other uses. For example, hyssop, which belongs to the mint family, is used in cooking, as a medicine, for its aromatic oils and for decoration.

**HIV** — see **AIDS**

**immunization** — giving a vaccine against a disease.

**incision** — in surgery, a cut made into a tissue or organ.

**infection** — a disease resulting from bacteria or viruses or other parasites.

**influenza** — often called 'the flu,' an infectious disease caused by a virus. No medication can cure it because a virus cannot be eliminated with drugs. The patient has fever, chills, sore throat, headache, cough, and achiness.

**inoculation** — a needle or pill that contains a small dose of a disease so that the body can build up a resistance (or immunity) to that disease.

**inpatient** — a patient who has to stay in the hospital or clinic while receiving treatment.

**intensive care unit** — ICU; a place in the hospital for patients requiring special, ongoing attention and care.

**intern** — a doctor who has just graduated from medical school and is serving one year as an apprentice in a hospital.

**labor** — the process of childbirth, including the contractions that lead to birth.

**malaria** — an infectious disease caused by a parasite, passed to humans by the bite of an infected female mosquito. Malaria is mainly found in the tropics and subtropics. The patient has headaches, chills, joint pain, fever, and sweating.

**malnutrition** — poor nourishment that can lead to health problems. Even people who eat a lot can be malnourished if they do not eat a well-balanced diet.

**measles** — an infectious disease caused by a virus that leads to a high fever and a rash. A vaccine to prevent it is available in wealthier countries.

**midwife** — a woman whose work is helping women in childbirth.

**mortality rate** — the rate of death, or the number of people who die from a certain thing.

**obstetrician** — a physician who deals with pregnancy and the delivery of babies.

**operating theater** — an operating room, where surgery takes place.

**outpatient** — a patient receiving treatment at a hospital or clinic without having to sleep over.

**pathologist** — a physician or scientist who specializes in the changes in organs and tissues caused by disease.

**pediatrician** — a physician who specializes in the health and illnesses of children and adolescents.

**penicillin** — an antibiotic that kills certain types of bacteria.

**pneumonia** — an infection of the lung.

**polio** — a contagious disease caused by a virus that attacks the central nervous system, hurting nerve cells that control muscles. The patient suffers paralysis of legs and problems with muscles. Vaccine is available in wealthier countries.

**postnatal** — the time immediately after the birth of a baby.

**prenatal** — the time during which a woman is pregnant before the birth of her baby.

**psychiatrist** — a physician who specializes in the diagnosis, treatment, and prevention of mental disorders.

**radiologist** — a physician who specializes in the use of x-rays, CAT scans, and MRI (magnetic resonance imaging) for diagnosing and treating diseases.

**resident** — a graduate doctor who is studying a medical specialty, usually for four or five years following medical school.

**ringworm** — a contagious skin disease caused by a fungus. The patient suffers itchiness, with ring-shaped patches covered with scales.

**scabies** — a contagious skin disease caused by a parasite mite that burrows under the skin to deposit eggs. The patient feels intense itchiness.

**sterilize** — to clean, or free from living organisms by using heat or chemicals.

**sulfa drugs** — a family of drugs used to fight certain bacterial infections.

**surgery** — an operation performed by a surgeon.

**sutures** — stitches made by a surgeon when joining together two edges of a wound or incision.

**tetanus** — an infectious disease, often fatal, caused by a bacterium that enters the body through wounds. Also called lockjaw, because certain muscles become stiff, especially in the jaw, face and neck.

**tuberculosis** — TB; an infectious disease caused by a bacterium that attacks the lungs. The patient has fever, night sweats, weight loss and may cough blood.

**undernourished** — eating less food than is needed for health and growth.

**vaccine** — a preparation given to a person (usually through a needle) to build up an immunity to a certain disease so that they will not get that disease in the future. There are vaccines available to prevent 11 childhood diseases. Listed are the diseases and the year in which each vaccine was introduced: diphtheria, 1923; pertussis (whooping cough), 1926; tetanus, 1927; polio, 1955; measles, 1963; mumps, 1967; rubella (German measles), 1969; hepatitis B, 1981; Hib meningitis, 1985; chicken pox, 1995; and pneumococcus, 2000.

**virus** — molecule that shows no sign of life until it enters a living cell, called the host. Human diseases caused by viruses include: the common cold, influenza, AIDS, cold sores, rabies, and many others.

**whooping cough** — an infectious disease of the respiratory (breathing) system, caused by a bacterium. The patient has violent attacks of coughing and bronchitis.

**worms** — a disease caused by parasitic worms in the intestines.

# ✪ Sources ✪

### EMILY STOWE

McCallum, Margaret, *Emily Stowe*. Canadian Pathfinders Series. Toronto: Grolier, 1989.

Ray, Janet, *Emily Stowe*. The Canadian Series. Toronto: Fitzhenry and Whiteside, 1978.

Waxman, Sydell, *Changing the Pattern: The Story of Emily Stowe*. Toronto: Napoleon Publishing, 1996.

### SUSAN LAFLESCHE PICOTTE

Ferris, Jeri, *Native American Doctor: The Story of Susan LaFlesche Picotte*. Minneapolis: Carolrhoda Books, 1991.

Additional sources can be found on the internet.

### MATILDA EVANS

Smith, Jessie Carey, *Notable Black American Women*. Detroit: Gale Research, 1992.

www.scafam-hist.org (South Carolina African American History Online)

www.mcphu.edu/institutes/iwh/whe/briefs/brief8.htm

www.thestate.com/packages/black/docs/evans20.htm

### MARIA MONTESSORI

Kramer, Rita, *Maria Montessori*. Oxford: Blackwell, 1978.

O'Connor, Barbara, *Mammolina: A Story About Maria Montessori*. Minneapolis: Carolrhoda Books, 1993.

www.montessorikids.com

Additional sources can be found on the internet.

## JERUSHA JHIRAD

Hellstedt, Leone McGregor, ed., *Women Physicians of the World: Autobiographies of Medical Pioneers*. Washington, DC: Hemisphere Publishing, 1978.

Jhirad, Abigail, *A Dream Realised: Biography of Dr. Jerusha J. Jhirad*. Bombay: ORT India, 1990.

Moses, Ezra, *The Reform Jewish Movement in India*. Toronto: Self-published, 1999.

Personal communication with Ezra Moses, Diana Mingail and Ann Samson, all of Toronto, Canada.

## LUCILLE TEASDALE

Arsenault, Michel, *Un reve pour la vie: une biographi de Lucille Teasdale et Piero Corti*. Montreal: Libre Expression, 1997.

www.lhospital.org (St. Mary's Lacor Hospital website)

www.aahsr.org/friends/01_ini/right/right_04a.html

*Dr. Lucille: The Lucille Teasdale Story*, film by George Mihalka.

## JOY SEAGER

Seager, Joy, *Kangaroo Island Doctor*. Anstey, Leistershire, UK: F.A. Thorpe, 1993.

www.atn.com.au/sa/south/towns-a.htm

Personal correspondence with Ray Swanson and Joan Huxtable of the National Trust Museum at Penneshaw and the Penneshaw Maritime and Folk Museum, Kangaroo Island, Australia.

## FE DEL MUNDO

Hellstedt, Leone McGregor, ed., *Women Physicians of the World: Autobiographies of Medical Pioneers*. Washington, D.C.: Hemisphere Publishing, 1978.

Personal communication with Dr. J.A. Aquino Sr. of Halifax, Nova Scotia, Canada.

Additional sources can be found on the internet.

## CAROLLE JEAN-MURAT

www.drcarolle.com
www.medalia.net/Hhistory.html
Personal correspondence with Dr. Jean-Murat.

## NADINE CARON

www.weq.gov.bc.ca/heritage/97/caron.stm
www.publicaffairs.ubc.ca/reports/97may22/nadine.html
Medical Post, volume 34(34) October 13, 1998, page 25.
Medical Post, volume 34(10) March 17, 1998, page 5.
Maclean's magazine (Toronto Edition) volume 110(26) July 1, 1997, pages 90-93.
Montreal Gazette, June 2, 1997, page E3.
Canadian Medical Association Journal volume 157(5) September 1, 1997, page 502.
Personal communication with Dr. Caron.

## GENERAL

Bailey, Brooke, *The Remarkable Lives of 100 Women Healers and Scientists*. Massachussetts: Bob Adams, 1994.
Macksey, Joan and Kenneth, *The Book of Women's Achievements*. NY: Stein and Day, 1975.
Stille, Darlene, *Extraordinary Women of Medicine*. NY: Children's Press, Grolier, 1997.
Ward, Brian, *The Story of Medicine*. London: Lorenz Books, 2000.

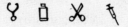

# ✪ Photo Credits ✪

### Cover
Oval portrait — Courtesy of Archives and Special Collections on Women in Medicine, MCP Hahnemann University, Philadelphia, Pennsylvania, USA.
Other photographs courtesy of the Lucille Teasdale and Piero Corti Foundation.

### Emily Stowe
Page 11 — Courtesy of Norwich and District Archives, Norwich, Ontario, Canada.
Page 15 — © Canada Post Corporation, (1981). Reproduced with permission.

### Susan LaFlesche Picotte
Page 19 — Courtesy of Archives and Special Collections on Women in Medicine, MCP Hahnemann University.
Page 23 — Courtesy of Hampton University Archives, Hampton, Virginia, USA

### Matilda Evans
Page 27 — Illustration from South Carolina African American History Online (www.scafam-hist.org).

### Maria Montessori
Page 32 — Courtesy of Kim Hunt, Creative Children's Montessori School, Toronto, Ontario, Canada.
Page 34 — Courtesy of the Montessori Archives.

### Jerusha Jhirad
Page 40 — Reproduced with kind permission of the Medical Women's International Association.
Page 47 — Courtesy of Ezra Moses, from the book *A Dream Realised* by Dr. Abigail Jhirad (Bombay: ORT India, 1990).

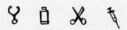